Two X Chromosomes with an Extra Shot of Melanin

Two X Chromosomes with an Extra Shot of Melanin

By Dara Kalima

Copyright © 2018 by Dara K. Marsh.
All rights reserved. This book or any portion thereof
may not be reproduced or used in any manner whatsoever
without the express written permission of the publisher
except for the use of brief quotations in a book review.
Printed in the United States of America

Cover by Dara Kalima

First Printing, 2019

ISBN-13: 978-0-9985020-1-4

For permission requests contact the publisher at: darakalima@gmail.com

Dedication

This book is dedicated to my angels Tank, Little O, Klassy K, Trace, and to my many ancestors.

This artistic expression is also dedicated to all of you who find yourself living at an intersection facing a myriad of oppressive paradigms. You are enough!

Forward

In a small Bronx classroom, on a warm afternoon in 1992 during my first year of teaching, I invited a group of 12- to 13-year-old girls to be a part of our school's first club designed to support and uplift the voices of our girls. As our club grew, we laughed and cried and laid a foundation for honoring young women's voices and explored what it would mean to excel as a Black woman. Dara Kalima was one of those trusting 12-year-old girls. Over time, my career took me out of the classroom and into a succession of leadership roles in the social sector. I went on to be CEO of a few nonprofits, and to co-chair New York City Council's Young Women's Initiative – an effort that brought policymakers, advocates, service providers, and researchers together with young women to improve the lives of young women and girls of color.

Over the years, that same hopefulness I had as a young teacher in the Bronx about the power of Black women persisted. And, somehow, as Dara navigated the trials and tribulations of high school, college, grad school and beyond, what emerged was an important friendship between two Black women whose mutual admiration for each other has grown. I have watched her struggle to find her voice, and then relished the moments when she finally felt understood, felt heard. Always, we both knew that this Black woman journey was going to be filled with highs and lows; and, that sometimes, the lows would bleed into the highs. There came a point where all I could offer was friendship – I still haven't figured out what a mastery of our shared identity was or looked like. So when I got a text asking me to write this introduction in the midst of preparing for my first ever TED Talk at TEDWomen 2018, I knew I couldn't say no.

Two X Chromosomes with an Extra Shot of Melanin won't solve our pain, we've got to do that healing work – but, I nodded throughout my reading. I saw myself in each love note and in every salty sweet word. Regardless of age or status, it is clear that Black women are in this thing together. This collection takes us on an exploration of privilege, police persecution, clutter, predatory student loans, and the generational trauma we've inherited from the American system of chattel slavery. Through the pain Dara reminds us of her magic and resilience and her never-fucking-giving-up-ness. Her poetry, like her life, is neither all black nor all white; villains and helpers come from all directions. The truth is that the reality of us spills out beyond childhood and peeks through at work, in our relationships, and takes root in our very wombs.

In this tome, Dara releases her frustration, and the pain that bubbles over when others empower themselves to define us, to control our bodies, to control our expressions of self, to control and/or silence our voices. In some ways, it's a coming of age story because she explores everything from the awkwardness and isolation of adolescence to the seemingly insurmountable hurdles that women face, like those experienced by Hillary Rodham Clinton. Like Dara expresses in one of her poems, I went from zero to C-cup seemingly overnight – and, it was the greatest threat to my childhood. She captures the nuance of the Black woman's experience in America brilliantly; invisible, and yet hyper-sexualized, inconsequential, and yet highly scrutinized. No, they ain't checking for us – but, yes, they're judging us – and our names and voices are forever in their mouths.

Words are important because life is complicated. Dara knows words. She shares her voice with us and for us. If you've ever wanted to scream from the top of a mountain and then come down more determined to keep going but can't find the words – Dara is your megaphone.

Written by Dr. Danielle R. Moss

Note from the Author

I stared at the TV in November 2016 with bated breath; the climate in the United States slowly became even more toxic as each state declared their winning candidate. The high from possibly electing a woman to be president fractured into rubble; a man who saw no shame in grabbing women by their genitals was elected to the highest office. It was painful to witness but from this loss, much was birthed.

As a rallying cry against the new administration and in defense of women, feminists vowed to descend upon DC to protest in January 2017. This call to action was not without issue, as the all white leadership tried to co-opt the name of a historic black women's march. The black community cried foul and demanded changes be made; the march needed to acknowledge the different plights of women, whether trans or cis, whether of color or white, whether living with disabilities or able-bodied. The only way this movement would work is if it honored all voices.

And it was in this moment, I learned about the term intersectional feminism. I often explain this term to people this way:
- If you a woman, you are oppressed by the patriarchy
- If you are a black woman, you must fight both men and racists
- If you are a black woman who is trans, now you must add transphobic folks to the list
- If you are all the above and living with a disability... well, you get it.

This is what the black community initially asked for; the movement had to acknowledge that oppression is compounding. And to combat it, we must rally behind those with the most complex oppressions, that is if we really want a truly equitable society.

Once the leadership of the march started to look more diverse and was now being led by women I'd been following for years, I committed to attending the march in DC, though there was one to happen at home in NY. During the march I noticed something fascinating; I was usually the only one in my immediate area demanding that people acknowledge that black (women) lives mattered. My fist would be the only one in the air, my voice would be the only one in agreement. I and a few others also observed that when one of the speakers who happened to be a trans woman took the stage, the audience around us stopped paying attention. We leaned in, while many tuned out. They could have been antsy, but I'm just not convinced that was what it was. It seemed as if cisgendered white folks didn't really care about more marginalized groups. Was this movement about to match the feminist waves of the past where black women were to bolster numbers only? Was I still not really invited to the conversation? I returned home with these questions.

In 2018, I decided to go the NY march with a group of activist friends. I was met with a lot of backlash from friends in the black community. How dare I support a white women's movement? Didn't I know it wasn't for me? How dare I show up to this march when these people were no ally to us? I was made to feel like I was betraying my race by aligning myself with white women, despite the fact that much of the leadership of the national movement was not actually white.

I went because I am a woman. But my race and plight were not to be ignored. I made a sign that spoke to my black woman intersection. I carried it proudly and then posted about my experience at both marches on an online feminist forum. In this group I was greeted with lots of deflection, fragility, and a few accusations. While some came to my aid, it saddened me that I needed assistance at all. My truth was either an exceptional experience or one to be dismissed. My story was always relational and could not just stand on its own.

So I picked up my pen and began writing poems exploring these experiences. Somehow I had to address the complexity of what it meant to be black and a woman in a world that seemed to demand I only identify as one. To align with women was to deny my blackness. To align with blackness was to deny my gender. I couldn't just be me.

In time I wrote the poem "What It All Means" where I speak about the experience of being both a woman and a black person. I highlight the oppressions felt and dealt by both sides. The hook in that poem, "two X chromosomes with an extra shot of melanin means..." led to the title of this book and provided its structure. Each section in this book has some version of this poem.

But in wanting to own my own voice, it was brought to my attention I was sending a transphobic message. I sat with this for months, grappled internally, and then reached out to two of my friends who happen to be trans. I take their opinion very seriously. And thankfully they did not hold back. The hurt the title caused was clear. See, people tend to use their incomplete understandings of gender, biology, and even sexuality to trap and exclude others they do not understand. To this community my use of two X chromosomes as synonymous with "woman" can be viewed as excluding too many and including some who don't see themselves as such. I can be seen as gatekeeping. I sat and listened. Over a series of days and messages, we discussed both my intent, the offensive impact, and just the terrible climate in which we currently reside. I dabbled with a different name, I debated with myself and with them as to how to address this concern while still honoring this body of work. The last thing I wanted to do was to hurt this community.

But what also became clear to me is that this book, while at times coming from a macro view of society, is really about my experience and ponderings about life at this particular intersection. This is my story and my truth. Nowhere in this book do I define what woman is, in fact I suggest a woman is what she defines herself to be. Not all women have two X chromosomes and not every person with two Xs is a woman. However, as a cisgender black woman, I am within my right to talk from this perspective. Like my existence, my truth won't make everyone happy, but it is mine to share. And so after much deliberation and contemplation, I have decided to stick with this title.

Make no mistake though, do not think that I am insensitive to the concerns shared with me. At some point I debated adding an additional section to address this, but thought it would be disingenuous for me to speak from any other perspective. There are oppressions, fears, and concerns which I cannot begin to understand. I'm wise enough to know that this topic far exceeds my understanding. It is not mine to discuss.

What is as true today as it was yesterday is that my activism is for all. I have and will continue to speak for others when they are not in the room, and will work to make space for them to speak when they are, should they choose to. I will support and help in any way that I can any writer who wants to share their narrative from their intersection. I will amplify their voice. I want to be a better ally than what I have experienced. I will make mistakes, I will try to do better. And I will stand up to allies demanding that they too do better.

Though I acknowledge this book title and the poems within the pages are not easy, and could be polarizing and possibly exclusionary, this book is my voice, my testimony, and my truth. I hope all who read it, learn from it, are challenged by it, and do better because of it. But I also hope this book and this note encourages readers to seek out and amplify the voices of all marginalized people. We will only be better, when we do better.

Yours in the movement.

Acknowledgements

I give honor, praises, and gratitude to God for blessing me with the gift of writing, the ability to use my hurt and curiosity for poetic expression, and giving me the tools to share it with others.

I must also take the time to acknowledge the many people that supported this poet and the creation of this book.

Thank you to my mom, Darlene, and dear friends, Corinne and Meg, for reading through the poems, providing edits, and feedback. And thank you Danielle for being my teacher, mentor, and friend and for the thought provoking introduction.

Much appreciation extends to my father Arthur and my brothers Cairo, David, and Ray for encouraging this artist. And I thank Sapphyra, Ena, Kameron, Nadia, and Tracey for giving me a reason to want to make the world a bit better through words. This sense of gratitude also extends to my mentees: TR, VT, SD and GC.

Special thanks to all my fellow writers and poets who have penned with me, challenged me, inspired me and given me a space on their stage to perform; this includes but is not limited to Bobby Gonzalez, J.P. Howard, Mike Geffner, Mo Beasley, the Black Authors Collaborative, the College Club Crew, and The New York Writing Club.

Thanks to my supportive circle: Alaya M, Amrita S, Catherine M, Catherine S, Chinwe E, Courtney N, Danielle CS, Emily M, Jamar M, Jenique J, Jerry F, Jessica M, Jim M, Jose E, Julius J, Kesi G, Kimma B, Michael M, Omar P, Paco I, Ramon G, Subha R, Symone E, Talib H, Tammy L, Tia F, Veronica M, and my Alaska, Journey, Momentum, NUL and PSN families. I also thank my loving family, my dear friends, and colleagues who let me test out my work on them or have inspired me along the way; I cannot name you all but believe me when I say the appreciation runs deep!

I hope you enjoy the book and find yourself challenged by it.

Contents

Preface
The Intersection ... 1

XX Chromosomes
Two X Chromosomes ... 4
my awkward phase ... 6
...But She Thinks She's Only Cute ... 6
Definition ... 8
Spherical Obsession ... 8
Her Unspoken Reality ... 9
How many children do you have? ... 11
Childless ... 12
Haiku on Being a Woman ... 13
The Closet ... 13
Trapped in a Binary ... 14
Slut ... 15
Who I Get to Be ... 16
The Fragrance of My Love ... 17
Rhythms ... 18
Ride of Shame ... 20
Consent Betrayed ... 20
His Happy Wife ... 21
Warning Label ... 22
Price Tag ... 23
Double Standard ... 23
American Gladiators ... 24
Broken Nail ... 25
Course Correction ... 25
My Swollen Feet ... 26
Through the Soiled Window ... 27
For 11 Minutes ... 28
The Hoarder ... 30
Observation ... 30
The Meeting ... 31
Majority Voices ... 32
A Constitutional ... 32
Why the #daywithoutwomen protest matters to me
    and should to you ... 33
Lines a.k.a. Signs ... 34
Majesty ... 36
Taking my dice ... 37

An Extra Shot of Melanin

My Name	40
America's Prepubescent Declaration	41
life's lessons	42
Haiku on Being Black	44
What Year Is This?... Still Being Sold	45
Black Privilege	46
What is privilege you ask?	47
The Removal of 'Some' From Vocabulary	49
Women's March	50
Salty Weapons	50
Stuck in the Past	51
An Ongoing Commentary	52
Intelligent Conversation	53
Bound Destinies	53
We've all been played...	54
2016 Black Reality	55
Redlines and Calculations	55
Flint	56
Saturday Morning Optics	57
Brown Bodies: Thursday, July 7th, 2016	57
How Many More?	59
The Crossroads: Get or Get Got	60
victim	64
How many cases you got?	65
Kamal	65
Ambien: Late Night Decisions	67
A Question Was Posed	70
Small Talk	70
An extra shot of melanin means	71
An Interpretation	73
A Farewell Letter	73

What It All Means

Morning Greeting	78
Split-Identity in a Minority War	79
So Much to Tell	79
A Black Woman's Plight	83
Fibroids - A Black Woman's Strength	84
Statistically Speaking	85
Half of Me	86

Tone Policing	87
Working while black	87
Entitlement - A New York Story	88
A Privilege I Do Not Have	89
Micro-Isms	90
Futuristic Fiction	91
Still Can't Win	92
I am tired.	93
Prayer Chain	94
Dear Self	96
A Gold Star Day	98
Haiku on Being a Black Woman	98
Korryn's Final Stand	99
No Comparison but Similar Still	101
The Answer is No	103
Rachel's Privilege	104
Turn of Fortunes	105
To John M	106
Why I Can't Date White	107
Why am I still single?	108
The Odds	109
But Do You Hear Me?	111
Happiness	115
As a Child	116
Vitiligo	117
Thoughts on Colorism	119
Black Girl Magic	120
Silver	122
What It All Means	123

Epilogue

Black and Women	125

Preface

"The Intersection"

Right below the part in her
glorious and righteous fro
is a fissure in her dome.
Her skull is cracking.
She is splitting in two
from the stress and
tension caused by
opposing forces that
require only parts.
Like a paper doll caught
in a childish and political
tug of war match,
she is slowly
being ripped in half.
And she screams in anguish
while fighting to stay whole,
fighting to stay complete,
but remaining intact and
autonomous is simply
not allowed. She must fall
in line on one of the sides,
there is no negotiation,
no compromise. She as is,
cannot serve their purposes
and so they pull. Back and
forth, they pull. Viciously and
selfishly they clutch and snatch;
both demanding that she be
their pawn, both needing her
to increase their numbers
and serve as their resource.
What she wants, matters not.
It is inconvenient for either
that she exists in the intersection.
She is either a black person or
a woman and must either
stand with black men
or march with white women,
despite the fact that she

straddles both, she is both,
and wants to honor
both, concurrently.
She can not.
There is no middle ground
even if she is the middle ground,
she cannot be allowed to stand her ground.
So they tug at her, like the pawn
they see her as, tearing her apart,
until something gives,
not caring if that something
is not just her crown, not caring
that what might be lost is
her sanity.

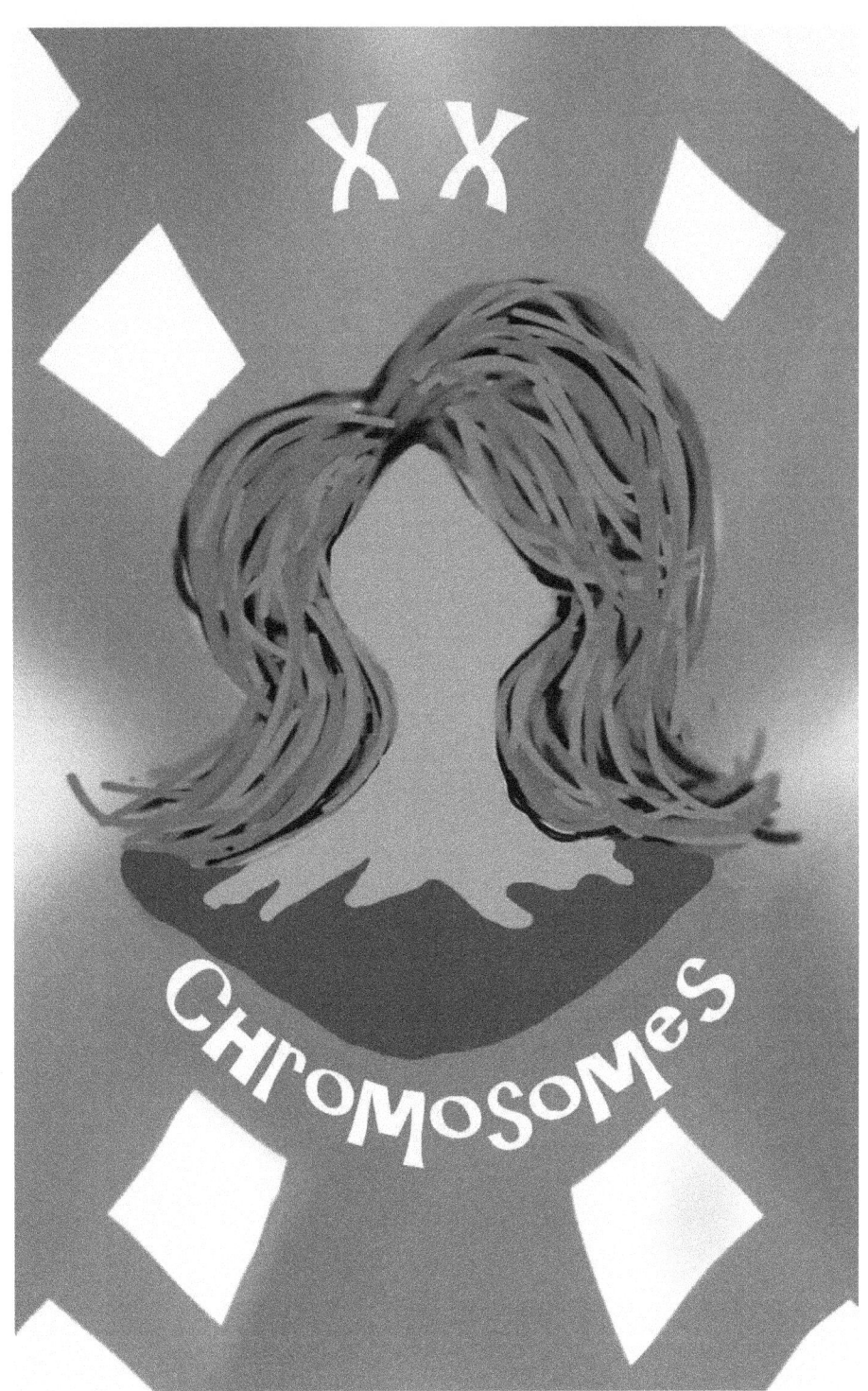

"Two X Chromosomes"

Two X chromosomes means
celebrating when leg, underarm, and pubic hairs grow in and then being shamed into removing them.

Two X chromosomes means
being picked on at 11 for not having breasts and then being preyed upon at 12 when they fully develop.

Two X chromosomes means
being expected to give birth and by a certain age, even if your body can't reproduce or you just don't want to. It's losing the right to choose because some with XY's decided that they know what's better for you.

Two X chromosomes means
being blamed for getting pregnant though it took two to conceive, you are the whore, not he. It's at best accepting the role of single motherhood if he denies your child and at worst it's being murdered for insisting on having it.

Two X chromosomes means
being told to cover up at work and church but then being told you must show the goods off if you want to attract a mate.

Two X chromosomes means
being taught to keep your legs closed and ankles crossed like a proper lady so he can manspread into your space.

Two X chromosomes means
being convinced to vote against your individual needs because your husband's financial interests trump all.

Two X chromosomes means
calling things boobs, boobies, tatas, the girls, vajajay, hooha, kitty, aunt flow, my friend, and all sorts of cryptic infantile names for the comfort of others.

Two X chromosomes means
deflecting cat calls on the street and ignoring inappropriate "jokes" in the office. It's peeling hands off your body. It's repeatedly saying

"no" to insistent suitors. It's playing nice even if you don't want to because your livelihood or life can be at stake.

Two X chromosomes means
being grateful for the reduced paycheck when your male colleague got the higher pay. It's being the new female CEO and still making less than some men on the payroll. It's smiling when you get looked over for the promotion because the real negotiations happened at the cigar bar that you were not invited to.

Two X chromosomes means
never being sick. Masking your way through feminine pain. It's toughening up and always showing up because the first sign of weakness, any sign of weakness will confirm their suspicions that you are the weaker sex.

Two X chromosomes means
being called a feminazi and told your feminism is toxic when you are merely demanding a seat at the table, a place in Congress, equal pay, and the right to make choices about your own body.

Two X chromosomes means
being asked what you were wearing, what you were doing, why you didn't just leave, why you left your drink unattended, and being questioned about your entire sexual past when you finally get courage enough to say you've been molested, assaulted, or raped.

Two X chromosomes means
being force fed Barbies, Easy Bake ovens, dresses, kitchen sets, the color pink, ribbons and bows when all you wanted were toy guns, Tonka trucks, science kits, and worms.

Two X chromosomes means
being all things to all parties: a nurse, a mother, a partner, a lover, an advocate, an advisor, a therapist, a pillar, a model, a cook, a cheerleader, and so much more, so many more selfless roles applied to those born with a with little time to define for self, what it means to have two X chromosomes.

"my awkward phase"

was one of "chubby"
and "chunky" jeans,
oversized modest shirts,
four flat cornrows, and
being called young man
even when outfitted in a
religiously pleated skirt,
while my dark leg hairs
poked through the white
tights; my clothes were
always awkward.
my hair, whether relaxed
or curly was also always
awkward. i was always
awkward, never learning
comfort in my own skin.
others controlled
what my body meant,
how it was presented,
and dictated what it was
worth. my body survived;
my femininity did not thrive.

"...But She Thinks She's Only Cute"

My parents named me Beautiful
and despite this naming
I have always been labeled cute.
My round face seems to confuse people
and causes them to mislabel me.
Is it my plump figure that hinders me?
Or the fact that I've never tapped into that
sexy, come hither, do me now look
that women develop during their teens,
that seductive expression women
started practicing once they started bleeding?
I was too busy with school, acting,
and being a kid to learn how to
twist my face, soften my voice

and walk with a switch. Only in the most
intimate of moments, when I cannot control
my desire, does she come out but that is not
for the average to see. They see
round face, big smile, glasses...
They fail to see my name. And because
they fail, I have admittedly lost my way.

See my loving ex spent four years, my
ex man spent four long years showering me in
you're-so-cute's and you-are-so-adorable's
and I began to digest it. Began to believe
what everyone else seemed to see... I was
not a woman who could be sexy, who could
stop men mid step, men on bikes, in cars,
trucks, trains and planes with my beauty. I was
always the odd one out. In a circle of five
at the club, I always danced solo or was pitied
by the sweaty, sleazy, slimy guy. And though
I tried to be the vigilant rock, the ocean
of insults converted my esteem into sand.

And today I painstakingly try to glue, solder,
meld, melt, and mend the pieces together because
this journey has finally brought me to my name.
My parents named me Beautiful and each day
on this earth I share this beauty. I shine my
fluorescent smile, extend my strong hand,
stay a pillar for others to lean on, and always
thank the Almighty for everything. I have lost
so much during that latter part of this journey but
like that gospel song says, "I Won't Complain."

For years, for over four years, for more than 24 years
I was force-fed a description I didn't want. I ate it for
breakfast, brunch, lunch, supper and dinner. It was my
late night snack and the mint on my pillow... but
in my journey I have realized that I was not misnamed.
At 260 nor at 140 was I ever misnamed. My birth name
was not just a word, not just an appearance, it is
and will forever be my legacy. My name is Beauty.

"Definition"

High heels,
short skirts,
tight shirts,
lashes,
long hair,
bare legs,
curves,
glutes,
mammary glands,
ovaries,
a uterus,
a labia,
chromosomes
do not define
womanhood.

"Spherical Obsession"

I am obsessed with my breasts.
As you may have noticed upon looking at me,
that they are a prominent feature.
Upon stepping to the Mic one night
the host spoke on their size
as his form of an introduction to my poem.
While walking down the Manhattan streets one gent
felt compelled to simply say nice tits,
and as I explained that's not how you greet a lady,
he heard no words, being too busy staring.
I get it, my breasts are hard to ignore
And quite frankly, I too
am obsessed with them
but not how expected.
I worry about their health,
I worry as to whether they are
predisposed to a tragic family legacy.
Will one day these assets turn on me,
anchor me to the same fate as my kin?
I worry about them always, check them always
not because I love the way they feel in my hands

but to ensure that there's no lumps this month,
that I'm only feeling fatty tissue,
that I'm only ever healthy,
to ensure that there's no visible clues
to alert me about deadly changes.
I worry about them so much that by the age of 30
I've gotten them mammogrammed
and sonogrammed annually,
always the youngest in the room,
always subject to sticky slime and
unnatural pressure as doctors seek to find
any early enough warning sign, just in case.
These are the things I obsess about
when I think of my breasts.
So as you linger and joke about them
being my best feature and worry if they hurt my back,
know that my back is strong but I'm burdened still.

"Her Unspoken Reality"

In her grey shirt and black pants combination
she sits hunched over staring at the screen
pecking away at the keys hoping everyone
assumes she's super focused and/or in need
of new glasses but what she needs
is to be home today. Her lining is mercilessly
ripping apart creating estrogen lacking
headaches and pain down to her toes. But
she smiles and pecks on, though her fibroids
are causing such hemorrhaging that she
embarrassingly leaks through barrier after
barrier every two to three hours, hence
the attire; light pants tell tales, skirts don't
feel secure and tights make access harder.
When it is all too much, she reaches for
the highest strength over the counter placebo
in her drawer when she's realized her latest
product has failed again. She slyly grabs
the next one. Math on her brain, if Janet
takes 57 steps per minute and she's two
minutes away from the private stall how many

steps before feeling embarrassed, icky,
worried, of course this is controlling for pain
that slows her down as she uses more energy
to be upright. Then she does even more math.
If a box of tampon ultras come 26 in a box
and costs $16 and she bleeds through one
in 3 hours, on a cycle that is 5-7 days, how much
will this month cost her for being female? She
puts math aside, does what must be done,
then cleans the crime scene as best she can
so that no one knows how compromised
she really is. She sits back at her desk in her
black pants and gray shirt, she leans in towards
the scene then plasters on a painfully plastic
smile just to ensure she doesn't betray herself
at work. This is only day two, she thinks,
and then she thinks of women in prison
who don't have the luxury of products
and painkillers, or the girls in other worlds
who are forced to miss school… her sisters…
she's the fortunate one, and then the pain
increases in magnitude again…

"How many children do you have?"

I have three nieces,
two goddaughters,
many little cousins,
six mentees, and
three sizable fibroids
taking up residence
in my perfectly designed
and functional uterus.
There's no room for you
to be in it too, so would
you go mind your own
reproductive organs
and stop assuming
that as a woman with
melanin I must have
multiple kids with varying
dads or that I want either
in my already fulfilling life?

"Childless"

Her womb
an abandoned
toxic wasteland,
filled with damaged,
rusty, parts. It strangles
and devours life from any
would-be inhabitants. Nothing
vibrant, lively, or new would dare
try to reside inside this broken womb.

Her heart,
her heart is as
vast as the heavens,
once you think you've
experienced all that could be,
another galaxy of beauty exposes
itself. It is endless and large enough to
openly embrace all of the Earth's children.

She is a
childless mother,
embracing all of the lost
and loveless. She nurtures, supports,
scolds, guides and provides for others though
her body prohibits her from having the full experience.

"Haiku on Being a Woman"

Role wanted matters
Not. It is assigned based on
Other's opinions.

"The Closet"

In preparation for the momentous
January march, a struggling soul
stands before its closet contemplating.
A big decision must be made;
what form will this soul take?
With which skin will they enter the world?
Will it slide on the pink camouflage?
Should it drape itself in the suit that
bonds it to their protest kin, in hopes of
pretending to be united in pussy hats?
Or will the restless and angry spirit
wrap itself in brown skin so others are
forced to acknowledge its existence?
Does it show up in brown so pink allies
are reminded that this precious essence
will not be a tool for bolstered numbers?
Choosing brown means a secondary protest
as the bigger wave of pink protests
against the dominant blue; while choosing
pink means falling into place and silencing
part of self, masking part of self, denying
part of self for a moment of racial peace.
The struggling soul stares into the closet,
a choice must be made: which form will be
represented and presented on this day.
Will they choose black or a woman today?

"Trapped in a Binary"

Male or female. Pink or blue,
Never lavender, which is a mix of the two.

Trucks and cars or a new baby doll.
Forced to suck it up or free to bawl.

Sneakers or heels. Suits or dresses.
A stout crew cut or long flowing tresses.

Hard or soft. The boss or his secretary.
One or two earrings. Cowboy or fairy.

Reading the Hardy Boys or Nancy Drew.
Points or shame whenever you screw.

Woodshop or Home Ec. Doctor or nurse.
Football or ballet. Briefcase or purse.

"You better bulk up" or "you are too fat,"
Are messages sent, what's up with that?

I'm trapped in a binary, that I don't quite fit.
Assignment was girl, so it's the cards that I get.

Neither feel right, though my body is fine,
And there's not something wrong with my mind.

We must resist and mix up the dichotomy,
Based on one's own biological anatomy.

I just want the best of both of these things.
The goal is not queen, it's to live as a king.

"Slut"

Why have you called me a slut?
What gave you the right?
What is it about me
that makes you think I am one?

Is it because
I have curves that clothing hugs
and that I won't hide?

Is it because
onlookers stop to stare
and bear witness to this beauty
gracing the same space
in which they reside?

Is it because
I exude femininity you can't have
and have no right to claim?

Is it because
I have intimate knowledge
of my own anatomy
and the ways to pleasure it?

Is it because
I do Kegel exercises
and demand ribbed condoms
simply to heighten my enjoyment?

Is it because
You are intimidated by
my body count, afraid that
I will know more than you?

It can't possibly be because
I stick tampons inside of myself,
is that why you've deemed me a slut?

Then what is it?
Because with zero partners
or many one can still contract an STI

so that status can't possibly be why.

So why? Is it because
I simply didn't smile, say hi,
bat my eyes at your advances?
Is this title you labeled me with
only a reflection of how low
you feel in the wake of
my rejection?

Yes, I think that was it.
That must be why.

"Who I Get to Be"

Regardless of outside opinion
today I decide who I get to be.
I can be a lady, a tomboy,
a seductress. I can be a femme,
an AG, or nonconforming of either.
Today I can use makeup and
a football helmet, rock heels
after a skateboard ride. Today,
I can choose between a gown,
baggy jeans, a mini skirt or
a pantsuit. I can pin my hair up,
let the wind have its way with it or
braid it. I may choose to invite
several into my bed or keep it
as a personal sanctuary. I can
be wife, mother, daughter,
sister or sistah-friend. I can yell,
scream, laugh loudly or whisper.
I can be meek, shy, introverted or
I can be an extrovert who is stern
and authoritative. Today I may
work as a domestic engineer,
a CEO, a mechanic, artist,
model, teacher, captain or
dragon slayer. I can push up
my breasts, let them hang freely

or tape them down. The only
requirement of the day is
to be authentically me.

"The Fragrance of My Love"

The fragrance of my love
is not the floating rose petals
caught in a cool refreshing
breeze on a summer's eve
or the odd "feminine" perfume
wafting from a scented tampon
or the sweet smell of recently
eaten pineapples. The fragrance
of my love is slightly musty
with a dash of salt added
from a long sweaty day.
It's the scent of someone
who could not afford to or
didn't want to spend the cash
on the luxury purchase of a
pack of fresh wipes to keep up
with mainstream hygiene practices,
imposed only on women, but
instead it smells like one who
used dry hard paper to remove
residual waste and whose
God-given hairs still snagged up
just a bit of what was removed.
It's the smell of someone
right before or right after
she menstruates where
she's made to feel somehow
unclean though her body is
preparing for or recovering from
its monthly natural cleansing.
My love smells like someone
that didn't fall for the financial
fallacy of douching, stripping
away my body's own stable
pH balance. It's the smell of

someone who has been told
that she should not complain
and that she is not allowed
to acknowledge her pain, and
that in fact it shouldn't exist, she
must stop being persistent;
it's the fragrance of someone
who persisted. My love emits
aromas of hard work, of struggle,
of nature, of love, of reproduction,
of beauty. The fragrance of my love
is not for everyone, it is not meant
to attract just anyone; its pheromones
whet the appetite of only worthy ones.
My fragrance is one that radiates
some of this and all of this at any, given, time.
The hardship and victories resides
in a scent that testifies to all endured;
that is the fragrance of my love.

"Rhythms"

He said,
"stay still,
don't move,
I got this",
as if his job
was to dominate,
control, subdue
my love organs,
as if the sway
of my hips
produced a
disruptive rhythm
he could not match,
it was a perfect rhythm
he could not match.

He said,
"don't move"
as if I was only
to be a recipient
and receptacle
for what he thought
he was putting down,
what he thought
his hips had
the power to do,
what he could not do.

He said
"be still,
I got this"
as if my body
didn't know
what it needed,
as if he knew better
than me as to what
was needed.

He said,
"be still"
as if submission
were the only position
I could play as we laid.

I did not stay still,
I could not stay still,
I refused to stay still.
There was
far too much
power
in my hips,
in these hips
to reign it in
just for him.

"Ride of Shame"

Could it be
more of a
testament
to how you
capitalized
upon your
limited time?
A badge of
honor, of
sorts rather
than of
shame?

"Consent Betrayed"

It started hot and heavy enough.
Two adults consenting to let
passion take over. Both consenting
to lustful and lust filled safe acts.
Both parties trusting each other
with their time, their hearts and
their bodies. But was he worthy
of this trust? Did she know that
in between actions her safety net
was to be removed; that he'd performed
acts not consented to? Did she know
this lover was no lover at all but
a vile individual who didn't care
about the terms of agreement? Did
she know he thought so low of her
that he'd remove the sleeve? Give
her his disease or his seed and
betray her trust, her time, her
heart and body when he acted
without consent? But know,
it wasn't her fault. He was wrong,
solely to blame, hold head high
with no shame. He will pay and
better than him is coming her way.

"His Happy Wife"

He entered the home
An odd smell filled the air
It was the heavy odor of iron
He checked each room
Looking frantically for the source
Each time calling out
The name of his "happy" wife
Last stop the bathroom
He stared at the red tub
With a razor laying by the side
And began to scream
He asked God why
His eyes filled with tears
For his love now lost
Then as he reached for a tissue
To wipe his weepy eyes
Something fell to the floor
And there he found his answer
A stick with pink lines.
It was better to be gone,
than bear his spawn.

"Warning Label"

My body is not public property
My hair is not for you to pet,
My curves are not for you to ogle
My breasts are not for your nourishment
My skin is not for you to judge my worth by
My uterus is not your human producing factory
And my vagina is not for you to conquer.

I am not your property,
though I exist in a public space,
my body is mine, owned by me.
Though history, media, and privilege
may convince you otherwise,
I am worth more than you can ever pay.
My wealth far exceeds your capabilities,
even if you assume you have a right
over all things me,
even if you think you have the ability
to take it from me.
You have no power over this body.

Do not touch.
Beware of the wrath of the owner
Do not attempt to mishandle me.

"Price Tag"

Skirts,
Dresses,
Brassieres,
Petticoats,
Stockings,
Haircuts,
Razors,
Makeup,
Gynecologists,
Mammograms,
IUDs,
Injections,
Diaphragms,
Tampons,
Pads,
Cups...
More expenses
All on a lower wage.

"Double Standard"

I want to be
sick like a guy.
I want to be
afflicted with
a regular boring
old head cold
and be allowed
to self-quarantine
and left to wallow
in misery
like the plague has
fallen upon me.
I want it to be
acceptable
to take an
adulting time out
to be added
to the sick and shut in list

over some sniffles
and a cough
because
as a working woman,
I'm expected to
perform through
flus, stomach viruses,
severe hemorrhaging
and am expected
to gracefully smile.
But he,
he can sneeze
once and
be down for the count.
I want to be sick
like a guy.

"American Gladiators"

Cloaked in her most fortified emotional armor
she steps out her door and into the gauntlet
as if trying to survive the final elimination course
where balls are literally and figuratively thrown at her.
She fakes left and ducks to the right trying to avoid
the unwanted contact. She must also traverse
treacherous balance beams while not being
thrown off by the hellos, the smiles, the whistles,
honked horns, and piercing, searing stares. She
dives over the "let me speak to your boss" vaults.
She runs forward on the reverse pay treadmill
determined to reach victory. She hangs from fixtures
on glass ceilings using all her upper body strength
to peddle her way to the entrance until she falls.
And after being held for five seconds longer than her
competitor in the penalty box, she climbs unsteady
rope ladders trying to get to the top. And at the final door,
her choice is usually blocked by another determined
for her failure. But despite each barrier, she reaches
the end, reaches her goal even if not in the first slot.

"Broken Nail"

Why am I the one that must comply?
Why must I always be under your watchful eye?
Why can't you just leave me be?
You obviously can't mold me into what you would like to see.
Get over your daydream 'cause no one can possibly be,
What you have come to expect of me.
Yes I may seem like a prissy little girl
But you must first step into my world
To understand what my eyes see.
I'm more of a woman than you could fathom me to be.
Yes, I may cry over a broken nail
But in understanding why, you seem to fail.
Did you ever think that I had the right to cry
'Cause that may be the only thing right in my life?
Behind that bright red nail polish bit
Is a woman that's been through all types of shit
But you are too ignorant to try to see
Past the exterior of me.

"Course Correction"

Wanting to avoid the one who lurks,
paths are changed each morning
to prevent another encounter.
The "good morning" guy knows her route,
knows her time, and in a crowd
singles her out, demanding a response.
Rather than make waves,
or be exposed any further,
she takes the long way.

"My Swollen Feet"

My feet ache
Swollen,
Flushed with blood,
Shoes beaten
And worn
But no rest
Must progress,

My bloated hands
Filled with water
Retained
From all
The excessively
Straining work,
Forced to go on
Despite the awkwardness,

My racing heart
Pounding furiously,
Working overtime,
Triple time
For no extra pay
But merely
For survival.

Body
Pushed
To the grindstone
Working hard every day
Fighting away.

"Through the Soiled Window"

She stared out the soiled scratchitied window
Blankly gazing at the blurred stations and
Watching the steal dust covered tunnels.
She hoped this common activity would
Grant her invisibility to fellow passengers

But I saw her, I saw what she could not hide
I saw the thoughts of the Sudoku game
Played in her head while trying to prevent
Her body from betraying her secret and from
Exposing her humiliation. I saw the truth.

The red eyelids told all, told the hurtful story,
Showed the plight of a woman rushing home
Before the purest emotions streamed again
Rushing to where she was willing to indulge
The façade-ripping hurt that stained her eyes.

She stared out the soiled window, watching
The dust-covered tunnels praying for invisibility
But I saw her, I saw it all, the pain and sorrow
I needed to offer a word, a tissue, a free hug
But she desperately did not want to be seen
Instead a private prayer was prayed for her.

"For 11 Minutes"

For 11 minutes,
After they stopped her
for failing to stop
at a stop sign,
they failed to stop
themselves and
proceeded on.

For 11 minutes,
after supposedly
smelling weed and
finding none,
they found other ways.
more humiliating ways
to intimidate her.

For 11 minutes,
after throwing her
under the car and
making her
a contortionist,
they made an
example out of her.

For 11 minutes,
she was back
on the auction block,
her parts displayed
for the viewing
pleasure of others
as they sized up
her insides.

For 11 minutes,
they examined
her sacred vagina
as if it was a room
to ransack,
looking for weed,
weeding out her dignity.

For 11 minutes,
she endured
only a part
of what slaves
experienced
as the father
of gynecology
restrained and
tortured them.

For 11 minutes,
the officers
who were sworn
to serve and protect
raped her, they raped
her in front of people
and cameras failing
to protect her dignity,
failing to protect her
from the system
that devalued her.

They did this
for 11 minutes,
for two unjustified
misdemeanors.
For 11 minutes,
and for eternity,
they changed this
innocent black
woman's life.

"The Hoarder"

I have buried my feelings
among the piles of clothes,
bags of garbage, lines of
tchotchkes, and cluttered
calendars. I've built a fort
of rotting books, delivery
boxes and recyclables.
I've closed doors and made
excuses, keeping all at bay,
burying myself away. I've
built a wall that's crumbling in,
sealing you out, sealing in
my fate, a prison designed
so well I can no longer escape,
this is my life sentence
courtesy of you and the hurt
you gave; here I will stay.

"Observation"

He said she seemed less angry.
Is that the case or did she just
resign herself to her fate?

"The Meeting"

It was as if the thought
hatched in her brain,
took its first steps down her throat,
leaped out of her mouth
missed everyone's ears
and landed on his tongue
to better present itself during that meeting.

It was also as if a different thought
blossomed in her mind,
gracefully flowed out of her esophagus
began its skillful dance
only for him to draw the curtains
and shut off the lights
before its conclusion.

It was as if the creative juices
that poured from her mind
down to her eager hand
was expertly typed in his font
as he stood before them all
distributing her creativity as his.

It was as if she was invited to the table
but her perspective was to be left at home
or reclaimed for him to own.

"Majority Voices"

Hillary was proven incompetent by email servers
but James' personal email account was forgivable.

Though Dolores said it in her native tongue,
they only believed it when Barack exclaimed "Yes We Can!"

And no-one heard Tarana proclaim "me too"
but it was spoken in unison when Alyssa exclaimed the same.

The majority, mimicking lesser, seems to always prevail.

"A Constitutional"

It was 2 p.m. and the
microaggression meter
reached its peak
so rather than lose my cool
I thought of my grandmother,
grabbed my jacket and went for a
constitutional walk as rehearsal for
the day that I walk out those doors
and do not return,
but this will work for the moment
as I just look for new
experiences new sights and views
to bring me back to okay,
so I put one foot in front of the other
seeking new adventures,
better experiences, ones where
respect is on the agenda of the day;
I let my feet take me away
from the land of microaggressions
and blatant disrespect.
At 2 p.m. I went for a constitutional.

"Why the #daywithoutwomen protest matters to me and should to you:"

1 - I am a woman, a black woman at that.
2 - Twice in my career, white men were better compensated for the same job.
3 - I was overlooked for a promotion given to an external man in a woman's org.
4 - I have fibroids, an issue 80% of black women have. Fibroids can cause severe pain, hemorrhaging, infertility, etc. but if we complain we are dismissed for being crazy or hormonal.
5 - Because I'm tired of being told to smile, told to show more cleavage, to talk softly, or that my degrees are prohibitive to me finding a mate.
6 - Because the officer said my rape was buyer's remorse.
7 - Because my rapist said it wasn't rape; "[his] people don't rape".
8 - Because I have nieces, goddaughters and mentees who deserve better.
9 - Because as much as I wasn't a fan of Hillary, the sexist paradigms held against her were unpalatable and disgusting.
10 - Because my Jewish friends should be able to wear long or short sleeves or skirts if they want. My Muslim sisters should be able to wear or not wear hijabs in observance of their religion. And neither should be forced into it or be ridiculed for their choice to do so as well.
11 - Because whether I have a body count of 100 sexual partners or none, I shouldn't be called a slut or a whore.
12 - By freeing me from limited gender roles, you free up men to be who they are and not conform to unrealistic roles either.
13 - Because tampons, pads, cups, sponges, are not free and cost us a big portion of our income to not bleed all over everything.
14 - Because GYNs and mammograms are not as easily accessible to those in poverty and we are losing our clinics.
15 - Because I should choose what I do with my body, not anyone else!
16 - My breasts or butt should not make me a target for unsolicited touching. I didn't ask to be rubbed up on the train or be flashed while he handled business on the bus.
17 - Because this list is longer than I can numerate.
18 - Because though white women get diagnosed with breast cancer more frequently women of color have higher mortality rates. Black women also have higher mortality rates during childbirth. Something is wrong with our healthcare system…

19 - Because birth control matters.
20 - Because sex trafficking is still a thing and it shouldn't be.
21 - Because no is no, not maybe, not yes, not kinda, not *sure*... it's NO!
22 - Because equality is a right and is right!

"Lines a.k.a. Signs"

Woman 1:
She spent tens of thousands trying to erase the lines, the signs... She sucked, tucked, plucked, dyed, lifted, lasered and injected everything. She covered the lines, covered the signs with makeup, and masked it under shades, scarves, fancy doos and plunging cleavage. Her obsession with youth stole that same youth away. She faded during the time she squandered in trying to keep time...

Woman 2:
She giggled the smile lines into permanence and proudly flaunted her grays. She

reveled in every
change age would
bring her way. She
welcomed them
in honor of her
fallen friends
who will never
see these days,
who will never
experience these
extraordinarily
trite changes.
Each a new treasured
companion provided
testimony to her
accomplishments and
perseverance. Her
giddiness made her
the youngest and
jolliest of the two.

Question:
Which one are you?

"Majesty"

Often when I ride the train
I'm greeted by a familiar
stranger. She sits opposite
and stares intently, never
breaking her gaze, so I stare
in response. Her features
captivates me. She possesses
a strong silhouette, beautiful
high cheekbones, defined
and full lips, a firm and regal
look emoting an older vibe.
I imagine she resembles
her ancestors, evoking her
grandmother's sexy social
club look. With each station,
each illuminated stop, my focus
fades but returns even more
intently in between destinations.
I desperately need to know
the secret behind the majesty
she reflects. Maybe one day
I'll figure it out, maybe one day
I will have a long enough
subway ride with her.

"Taking my dice"

That's it, I'm done. I quit.
I'm not playing with you anymore.
You don't play fair!
And I no longer need to subject myself
to your ever-changing rules,
the moving finish lines,
and permanently rising ceiling
designed to keep me trying and failing.
You can play by yourself,
I don't have to join you.
I will take my magic,
my gifts, my talent,
everything I've contributed
to your game with me and
find ways to participate in games
where the odds are better
even if still not even.
I quit this game.

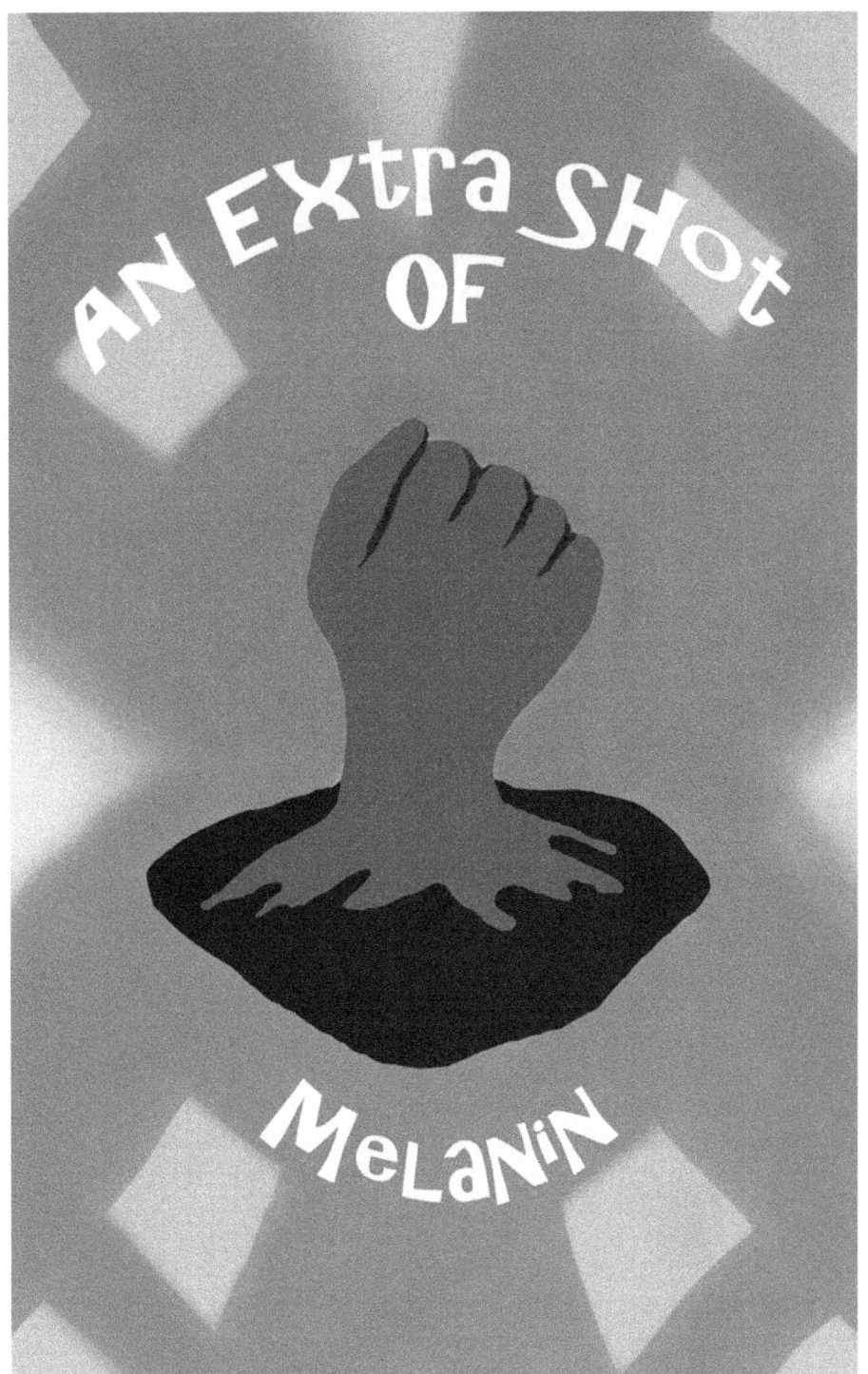

"My Name"

I am African American, not just Black or simply American… I am African American. I am African even if my memory does not extend further than the claustrophobic death-stenched ships. No, I do not remember what it felt like to be kissed by the African sun, or how my feet caressed the soil, I do not remember my native tongue, I forgot our celebratory dance and what our funeral rituals entailed. I am not even certain as to what part of the vast land I once resided on but I know that even with a million generations between us, my kin is still there. My African mother bore me, helped to bring me into existence and yet here you are today requesting that I deny that her blood still resides inside. You act as if my American father is the only one I am allowed to claim, as if his patriarchal rights not only supersedes but completely nullify hers. Yes, he snuck into her bed impregnating her belly, producing me, it took two. I am of both. Thieves stole me from mother's breast, imprisoned me, physically and then mentally raped me, beat me and washed me in Christianity to the point in which I forgot how to say my own name. My genes have been considered a crime punishable by the death of what you call unsightly, unkempt, nappy hair. My nose and lips made fun of for being "unnaturally" big but all I see is you trying to look like me, my natural brown skin a sin while you risk cancer trying to be bronze, and people inject chemicals into hips to get what I was blessed with… this is not to say that I hate my new home. The truth is I have no choice but to love it, yet it fails to acknowledge me as a citizen because Mother's imprint has yet to fully fade away. I am still of her, I am still of you, though denied by both. I am my own entity, an orphan of sorts. A child that never knew Mother and never completely won Father's approval, but do not pity me. I have my identity as a complex,

beautiful specimen of human with the blood of
royalty and leaders on both sides. I've known
both pain and loss, but also tasted the joys of
victory, I don't need pity or sympathy for my plight,
I am just fine but don't dare try to redefine this divine
entity I am. My mother is Africa, my father America
my name I carry with no shame… So I will say it
for the last time, I am not just black, and not
simply American, my name is African American.

"America's Prepubescent Declaration"

Though my veins
bleed red, black
and green, my heart
beats to the cadence
of red, white and blue.

I'm an unwanted child
of reluctant parents,
loving both for their
contributions despite
their contradictions.

Though here by force,
though never given
a choice, and while far
from free in 1776 or
in 2019, this particular
and peculiar parent
made me its child
and like all children
I too created parents.
And though, I despise
the neglect, the abuse
and the denial of my
existence suffered
at the will, and hands,
and tools of my lacking
progenitor, without its
persistence I wouldn't,

I couldn't possibly be.

I have no choice but to
own and acknowledge
the complexity of this
relationship, and I
salute my faulty parent
on the anniversary
of the day it declared
the end of its infancy
embarking on this
centuries long rites
of passage. May it
one day find itself
to be fully mature.

"life's lessons"

i wish that i could tell you
all of the lessons life has
taught me, i'd love to be
able to put my life on this
paper, let the pen tell all,
but i can't. every instance
in which i try, my vision
blurs, a knot blocks my throat
and aversion to pain reflexes
consume every future action.
rather than pen feelings,
i automatically, as if on
autopilot, instinctually
focus my energy on pain
reduction until i succeed at
pain avoidance. so the words
that tried to find liberation are
stifled, they get trapped in my
heart and stuck in my brain.

but i desperately wish that i
could tell you, that i could
get you to understand the

path to me, the lessons
learned, but i can't, it's too
painful. there's too much
pain involved in reliving these
moments just for your benefit.
even if it would after time
and distance, prove to be
healing for me, i'm too busy
maintaining my equilibrium.

but of the many life lessons
learned, i've finally learned
that it is in fact okay to cry,
but, not for too long, not too
loudly, and only up to three
tears are allowed to escape
before blame must be placed
on foreign particles irritating
the cornea, it has nothing
to do with emotions irritating
the heart, or memories irritating
the mind... it cannot be more...

and though i now know how
to cry, now that there's been
permission given on the
permissibility of tears, i also
learned that cry time must be
scheduled, it must be private,
and if it is not tears of joy,
you must be mindful of your
audience. that form of
emotional expression isn't
for everyone, not everyone,
not any one cares to see it.

so as i hold this pen, as i
look at this page, and as i try
to share my story i realize i'm
unable to because i'm so
preoccupied with trying not
to cry. there's too many
rules surrounding when

my tears are justified
and are classified as a valid
form of expression. there are
so many rules surrounding
my tears that i am too
preoccupied with being a
socially responsible law
abiding citizen to be able
to share the story behind
them with you. i am unable
to share my story still.

one day, i hope to tell,
i hope to be able to tell it
all, to turn it all over to
the page, and release
it into the world, but for now
my story will linger in a lasting
wish, one wish to one day
share all of my life's lessons.

"Haiku on Being Black"

Trauma so profound
Even when brown skin differs
We too feel the pain.

"What Year Is This?... Still Being Sold"

They ripped Mayan speaking,
Spanish speaking,
Non-English speaking,
not yet speaking babies
from their mothers
at a time when bonding
is necessary, at a time
when both need each other,
need each other to develop
and heal from postpartum separation
but they have been ripped apart
all in the name of politics,
scarring both in ways
that time will only show but
that time will most certainly show.
She aches for her child
with swollen breasts
and broken hearts,
unable to nurture and
feed the soul so dear to her.
She was stripped
of her parental rights
as they ripped the child away
who she only ever hoped
to give a better chance to,
to provide a different life to,
and now they will carry this imprint
of separation on their psyches for life.
This mother intended
so much good, tried for better
and instead lost it all.
With only hopes of
eventual reunification,
this is now her only dream.

"Black Privilege"

As a member of the community,
I reap the benefits of black privilege.
I hail cabs without being bypassed.
Though at times belligerent,
I survive police encounters.
Loans and interest rates are eased for me.
I get to live in the best communities
and take over the ones I want.
That CEO position is mine for the taking.
My generational wealth is secure
and even if I happen to struggle,
society doesn't consider my use
of public assistance the true problem.
Rehab is my main option when addicted
and I get 20% lighter sentences
if I am mistakenly imprisoned.
As a bonus my black privilege
gives me the right to be butt hurt
when others get similar opportunities,
how dare they take them from me?
I'm shown always in the best light,
and even if I do wrong, I'm an outlier,
my sin is not a detriment to my kin.
My black privilege means that
the hair care aisle and all beauty products
are made for me. In fact, naked and
nude are my perfect match.
I am the majority in every room and
can Columbus the ones in which I'm not.
I am never an "other" unless I choose it
and then, when fatigued, I can skip the fight,
my life isn't on the line after all.
I get to travel anywhere domestically
and internationally and be welcomed.
My privilege makes me the greatest
recipient of public policies like
the GI Bill, Affirmative Action and
even welfare. My beauty sets the standard,
my image is everywhere, it really is,
I even get to demand seats from others,
to feel safe in my skin, and get adopted first.

I have the privilege of being offended when
I can't use certain words against others.
My word is considered bond even
when I'm in the mood for bending truth.
I get to be oblivious about oppressions
and am validated in believing that
it's really oppressive to me, to be called
an oppressor... Oh... my bad,
that is not black privilege,
that is white privilege. As is forgetting
that most of the public policies
enacted to benefit me, not only benefit me
less but were also created to correct
for decades and centuries of wrong.
So yes, I may get a discount here and there
by my similarly hued fam, there may be
a secret nod of understanding but
the only real privilege I have
is that of being the wildest, best,
and unimaginable dreams of
Feliciana and Lucinda, my foremothers
who I'm certain couldn't imagine this day.
They survived slavery then so that I
can fight its systematic ancestor today.

"What is privilege you ask?"

It's being able to walk around in an open carry state
with an AK-47 strapped to your back as you get coffee
while a darker child in the same state holding a bb gun
gets gunned down in under 3 seconds.

It's finding humor in giving and videotaping little white girls
as they open black doll presents to see their tortured
response as if they were given a punishment as opposed
to a treasure while young black and brown girls
have to hunt and search for dolls that look like them.

Privilege is getting up in arms, going on social media tirades
and calling a broadcast of the all black cast of The Wiz racist
and questioning how people of color would respond if there was an
all-white cast, forgetting the Wizard of Oz existed first,
forgetting that this is the majority of their media... this is the
experience of people of color... always removed from existence...

Privilege is being able to walk into a public high school
in an affluent community and simply wave at security
while other kids in lesser than public schools start their day by
getting waved down with a wand by their school safety officers.

Privilege is getting on an elevator and having no-one
grab their bag when you step on, then tightly clutching
your purse when one who doesn't look like you next steps on.

Privilege is why armed men who take over a federal park
are called a "peaceful protest" or why college kids can ransack
a town because their team won, but when people of color
take to the streets armed with signs, demanding answers
as to why their skin is not legal, they are labeled thugs, their
protest called a riot, and national guards bring tanks to tame.

And privilege is telling me I need to not be so angry about
the status of my people and my life. It's saying never wear
dreadlocks, as braids are more acceptable, but straight is ideal.

To be privileged is to be the one to tell me or to believe
that I should whiten and lighten up and not demand
that my name be said correctly. And that in order
to get ahead I must be docile, graceful and forgiving.

The lack of privilege is to be told that I must operate
from love while others have free reign to hate. It is to be
told that my anger, my hurt, really that I, am not justified....

If this resonates with you, check your privilege
before I am forced to check you.

"The Removal of 'Some' From Vocabulary"

To say "some" and not all
lets the collective actors
off the hook and ensures
things remain status quo.
To say "some" denies
the monolith they are,
while forcing others into one.
To say "some" allows everyone
to think they are special
despite being part of the hive.
To say "some" allows for
a majority individuality
that the minority never gets.
To say "some" keeps predators
and perpetrators comfortable
at the expense of their victims.
To say "some" distances people
from the ways in which
they have been bred into it,
raised on it, benefitted from it,
and upheld it. To say "some"
is a cop out.
If some are comfy
with "some" it is because
they can remove themselves
from the equation and
can exempt themselves
from analyzing just how
complicit they are.
To say "some" is to
continue lying
about how large
of a problem it –
how large of a problem
systematic racism – is.

"Women's March"

He told her
not to attend.
In the game
called life,
Black
always
trumps
female.

"Salty Weapons"

She weaponized her sweaty eyeballs
that dripped with deception, with malice,
with privilege and made herself the victim
after she victimized him, lied on him,
imprisoned him, caused his lynching.

She weaponized her sweaty eyeballs,
knowing the manipulative power of her tears
building upon centuries of societal problems,
tapping into her legacy as oppressor,
and ruined his life out of spite, hate,
and simply because she could.

She weaponized her sweaty eyeballs
demanding justice for unjustified claims
her tears need be her only testimony
against any individual of darker hue.

"Stuck in the Past"

Today we fight with men and boys stuck in the past
glorifying past figures and statues. Reliving and
reviving an ancient tyrannical day. Today we fight
with men who fight for statues placed in another
time of tyranny in honor of great tyrants who lost
the battle, who were on the wrong side of history but
they keep memorializing them as if they were
the greatest people to be. Today we fight over these
symbols that to many mean oppression, slavery, rape
and abuse. They, on the wrong side, honor the ones who
glorify the worst of the past and they won't tell the truth,
don't tell the truth that the past was treacherous.
The placards speak to their honor and their glory
but they were never glorious, never honorable.
And today they are so stuck in the past, that they can't
get out of the past, can't see past the fairy tales told of
greatness, of stick-to-itiveness, of valor to see the truth
behind the tall tales. Their heroes fought only for greed,
to retain their profits earned on the backs of human
property. They espouse statements of purity when
15% of their DNA suggests otherwise, they deny and
rewrite truths when their own bodies betray them,
their own cells reveals the lies… but they are
caught in a past celebrating dead men, celebrating
statues erected to impose fear over 50 years post-
defeat, as if these monuments were monuments
of over compensations of what they lacked, what they
claim to want back, but never truly ever had.

The statues are untrue, the placards are untrue,
the stories of valor and greatness are untrue, but
while the world browns, they remain too stuck
in the past to see what's real and what will be
inevitably true, their reign of terror is through.

"An Ongoing Commentary"

Did you see?

                                  See what?

The windows!

                                Which windows?

The ones on 8th and D;
the ones that give you peek
into the soul of New York
and original sins of America.

                                You've lost me.
                         First windows now souls?

Three windows, in Alphabet City,
peering down onto the street,
brimming and beaming with
vengeance filled irises of red
and blue, a crisscrossed view
with 13 spangled stars…

                         They are here? Really??

They've made their presence known
In the heart of "diversity".

               First, they came for Virginia
                  and now New York has
                    become infested too…

But is this infestation really new?

"Intelligent Conversation"

We will never have an intelligent conversation.
Too many unintelligent things have been said.
Too many caustic words have been hurled.
Too many accusations have sliced away
any possible chance of communication.

We've buried ourselves in too much pain.
We've covered our hearts with our hands barring
The entrance or escape of compassion or sympathy.
We've even become unable to understand our own aches,
So how can we intelligently explain it to the other?

We've reached an impasse with nothing left to be said
We've shut ourselves in and locked each other out.
Rather than healing, rather than building a bridge,
We only complained, never learned how to listen.
Learned only to nurture our hurt, to nurture our hate.

Those complaints have become bitter balls of blame
That grew to the toxic weapons we spew today.
And we are now so busy trying to kill the other,
That we've managed to destroy all that there was,
All is destroyed because of our failure to communicate.

"Bound Destinies"

Subjugate is goal
You will learn your role
We're trapped.
Hate for skin of coal
You'll take what I dole
I've snapped
3/5ths never whole
You'll pay me the toll.
Enwrapped.

"We've all been played…"

We've been so well played against the other
that we fail to see how much we need each other.
Our situations make us akin to cousins, if not brothers.
And every time
we've tried to cross racial lines
the powers that be, put us back in our places
among homogeneous faces
so that we can't collectively demand our proper spaces.

Those with darker hues
with similar views
have always been villainized so that
it's better to be poor white than any category black,
allies convinced to turn their back,
for promises of economic slack,
missing the fact that
little ever changed for either,
the rigged system made to enhance neither,
but by using race as a ploy,
those with vested interests can act coy,
when called out on how they used us as a toy…

See the impact of greedy policies comes in waves,
crushing some immediately, others in coming days.
And the result being that we all suffer
when poor whites use those with color as a buffer.

So, let's stop falling for the distraction,
that prevents us united, from gaining traction.
You and I can no longer afford,
to not operate on one accord,
not if we truly want our livelihood restored.
So, I ask, are you finally onboard?

"2016 Black Reality"

It's the impact of reality
after hoping that once
you emerge from that
stifling stagnant stinking
station and climb those
treacherous stairs finally
ascending from the
summer subway to
achieving the same
level as others, in hopes
that you will be able
to breathe uninhibited,
the hope that the air
will in fact be fresher,
when you are instead
greeted with stuffy,
sweltering, staggeringly
oppressive heat…
It's the impact of hope
hitting a disappointing reality.

"Redlines and Calculations"

Retired red pens and wooden rulers
were replaced by computer calculations
justifying, with statistically sound reasons,
why loans must be denied or inflated
for a specific few, making them card carrying
members of debtor's prisons while others
without barriers blame their money mismanagement
on the victims without ever realizing
the upper hand they've been dealt.
Decades have passed, tools have changed
the policies are still very much the same.

"Flint"

They say that genocide is a thing of the past,
these campaigns ended with Nazi Germany,
acting as if this is some foreign concept
without ever acknowledging that the search
for the master race started here, the seeds
were sowed on this land. They say that
genocide is wrong, that we as a country
are above it though it's never made reparations
for the past built on the decimation of a people.
They say that genocide is done and gone
but they forget that even in recent history
her story is genocide, incarcerated black
and brown women were forcibly sterilized
in the name of their betterment. Wiping out
future lines, erasing legacies and lineage.
And folks still refuse to acknowledge that
the murder of black men at the hands of officers
is a genocide tactic... we are above genocide
but had the victims been white and wealthy,
there would be more outrage about the systematic
poisoning of 9,000 children in Michigan. Their
brown bodies were denied the basic necessity
of clean water. The water is measuring at
toxic waste levels in a town where most
of the residents are brown... no one
is losing their job for creating this crisis
though lives are being risked for a game
of monopoly... a community slowly poisoned...
a community slowly murdered... but
they say genocide no longer exists.

"Saturday Morning Optics"

He sat on the LIRR train with his
hood up, headphones on, bookbag
still on his back with a lunch bag
in the seat next to him. The police
stopped the train from departing,
questioned him about the lunch bag,
and asked him to disembark. He
complied with a tragically familiar
pain releasing chuckle. His tall
black frame stood with his arms
out, head slightly tilted looking
similar to the religious icon, with
five blue-clad officers surrounding him,
persecuting him. Many white
witnesses looked on. The optics
reinforced ideas of black criminality.

"Brown Bodies: Thursday, July 7th, 2016"

On this day the newspaper
put what was evident to many
on the front cover.
Alton's hands were empty.
His hands were empty,
when he was murdered by
armed blue hands that were attached
to blue bodies that were piled on him
moments before he was murdered.

On the cover of the paper was Alton's
brown body, bloodied, bare handed
lying there with the officer nearby
still pointing at him as he slipped away.

I hate this image.

I hate that while taking up this cause
on its cover, the paper too left his body exposed.
It was another brown body exposed.

Another brown body bloodied and vacant.
It's never a white body, always brown…

When the school in Africa was ambushed
and when the pictures finally reached the media
it was all brown bodies… but
a mixed population on 9/11 is documented
with buildings, smoke and hero pictures. But
when Haiti shook, mangled brown bodies
were crushed under concrete, we showed it all…
Yet a massacre at a Midwest workplace of
mostly white people only displayed
the building, the killer, no bodies…

No peach bodies… only ever brown…

Why are we still displaying brown bodies
like folks did at mass lynchings,
ropes were exchanged for chokeholds or
bullets but our bodies are still displayed
serving as soft porn for racists and
teaching deadly lessons for those
brown bodies that are still inhabited…

Why?

I saw the paper on July 7th,
but all I could see was the black
and white image displaying brown bodies
like fish plucked from the sea
as if there is no travesty.
And whether it was done to make a point
about a lack of evidence or
just to place another one on display,
what I saw fully and clearly
is that just like in life, brown bodies
will never get the same respect.

"How Many More?"

How many more, how many more names must we collect? How many more poems must be written? I don't think my heart can handle much more.

How many more police will not be convicted or even be indicted for murder? How many will have pensions subsidized by crowdfunding monies? How many more?

How many more times will we be gunned down in stairwells or chased through our own neighborhoods? How many more wallets and phones will be mistaken for weapons? How many more times will we have to scream that we can't breathe?

How many more of us will be stopped, frisked and summoned? How many more will be pulled over when driving down the street? How many more will be reported for looking suspicious when going for a jog or sitting in a coffee shop?

How many more stores must we burn? How many more businesses must be looted? How many more cities must be rioted?

How many more mothers will need to teach their sons how to survive interactions with the police? How many more will still not make it home?

How many more white men will wave guns at cops and camera men but still be allowed to walk away? How many more white women will yell at officers and also walk away? How many more black people will do the same and not survive the interaction?

How many more times will a toy gun justify the death penalty? How many more times will our babies be mistaken for the hulk?

How many more female victims will we ignore as part of this narrative? Sisters are not just the wives and spouses of these victims they too are victims! So how many more?

How many more times will we allow officers to lie to our face about what transpired? How many more times will we have proof and still wonder if they will be convicted? How many times?

We were up in arms about Diallo. We were disgusted by Bell. It happens almost every day. Martin, Garner, Brown, Graham, Gurley, Gray, Rice, Crawford, McKenna, Jean, Roberson, Bradford, Boyd, Bland... There so many names; I cannot recall them all... But I must recall them until there are no more...

And how many more "friends" must I lose because they can't empathize or even sympathize with my pain? How many times must I call for an ally and realize I am left alone? How many more? How, many more? How, many, more? Before change finally comes...

"The Crossroads: Get or Get Got"

I am permanently at a crossroads,
a walking contradiction,
a conundrum for some.
See, I am everything society created
and much of what they wish they could terminate.
I was born, statistically speaking,
to middle class parents but my zip code was
a block below the Bronx north-south border.
And even in my next more northern abode
I was still on the wrong side of the elevated tracks.
The benchmark for success always pushed back.
I am the product of an addict and a bible thumper.
I attended both private and public schools.
I got to college. Collected multiple degrees
then collected 72 unemployment checks
and for six months more, I lived off poured pennies
from a tipped savings jar aka a water cooler
that found itself in my possession.
It was my only valuable possession.
Now I technically earn a middle-class income
but I still live with mom because
that college dream and that predatory credit company
has my veins permanently
attached to banks that withdraw 3/5ths.
I know that with every next purchase,
be it food, clothes or tampons,
I could slip back through the cracks...
and yet I'm one of the success stories...

at the peak of where I'm allowed to be...

success......

Success is another moving target
because society only hired blacks for certain jobs
so my sky blue collared parents
were always trapped under a two-way mirrored ceiling
that I later inherited.
The have-nots can look up but
the reflection of self beaming back at those that have
is so bright they won't see the residents below
even though their stability is built on fragile glass.
But despite the fractures in my family foundation,
I was given choices and opportunities.
I knew I had agency even if minorly...
Three out of four of us kids made it out
with only bruises and debt
so it would be very easy for me to say
"well I did it so can you" to the guy sitting on my stoop.
"Shoot we all have choices, we all have opportunities so make something better"...
I could think this or offer them better but
fear of my brother often keeps me from opening my mouth.
Yes, they need a mentor but
if my successful brothers won't mentor my less so brothers
why would these guys listen to me –
a chick who will never ever fully understand
the difficulties of being a black man?
Though relatives, we can't relate.

So, I walk on by with my head lowered and my ears plugged
preparing to make magic tricks with my two cents...
such a product of the 'me first' mentality
I ignore the person in need who looks just like me.
I never tell them they have choices.
I never offer up support.
I join everyone else that ignores.
But they still have choices to make for good or for bad.
But not the choices, opportunities and agency I had
so how dare I fault them for making the best choice possible.
When offered a platter of 'get others or get got'
how can I be mad that they didn't get an education

or get a job instead,
especially when never given the tools to do so?
We so failed them, you know....

And did you know the other day
the police announced the biggest gang takedown in NYC?
My hood is now part of this ongoing story...
Two gangs.
100 people.
All black and brown.
Thieves, murderers, and
the all encapsulating "thug."

And admittedly I'm glad they are off the street
so my friend can take her child to the park
without fear of getting got for not
being properly associated,
for lacking the correct affiliation.
Yes, they should be locked up for crimes committed
but if the only thing we offered
is the same script we all see
"brown bodies belong in prison, if not dead on the street"
then aren't they simply fulfilling their preordained
publicly subscribed destiny;
a plan backed by you and me
when we looked down rather than engage,
when we skipped that community board meeting...
when we decided not to vote,
when we... when we...
when we...

And this question,
this dilemma, is where I reside.
I didn't follow that path of those arrested
but like them, I am still stuck under the floor.
Yet my choices allow me the privilege to judge,
it is so easy to judge. But why should I,
why would I, how could I?

I looked at the news and felt my contradiction.
I'm one choice away from being them,
one choice away from not,
and no chance at being more

because society has already gotten me got
even if not behind bars, if only under floors...
I'm privileged and disadvantaged.
I am permanently at a crossroads,
a walking contradiction,
a conundrum for some.

See, I am everything society created
and much of what they wish they could terminate,
though they haven't been successful at it yet.
I am on the wrong side of the elevated tracks.
I have options but still lack.
And I am one purchase, one mistake,
one misstep, one medical emergency away
from getting gotten or go getting...

And if I, a "success" story, am permanently
at a crossroads with many limited choices, then
what chances have my restricted kin?

"victim"

you scoff at the use of the word "victim"
when referencing convicted convicts
but they just might be the biggest victims
of a capitalist society that believes
that there is more financial benefit
when they lock potential behind bars.
the convicted are the victims of a country
that relied so heavily on slavery that it
enslaved those recently freed for eternity,
changing the justice system so that
cheap labor can be made of those
that walked the rails to opportunity.
the only opportunity afforded them
was a legacy of oppression. see,
the system has always been designed
along racial lines. laws contorted and
created to create a system, an industry,
that thrived on hope's demise.
from the moment they sprung
from between momma's thighs
the government's eyes were focused
on the potential that imprisonment
would have on their pockets... whether
the policy was vagrancy or stop and frisk
their future has always been at risk
so it is no surprise my brothers stay enslaved
because the world that bore them
would have it no other way. with no options,
crime became the only choice of brothers
who never knew the power of their voice.
but rather than call them victim, we label them
criminal because society said make it so...
but keep your heads up, fight to be better,
you can be you are more than criminal, more
than victim, you are hope and power and potential.

"How many cases you got?"

I've got one case
for my phone,
a case of the finest
African wine, three
briefcases for work.
I've had two cases
of the flu so now
I just get the shot.
I have two durable
Samsonite suitcases
that travel with me.
I still have over 200
CDs with dust
covered cases
and I've got 37 court
cases where I'm
defending wrongfully
accused folks,
so can you get off
my case and quit
assuming I have
numerous or any
criminal cases against
me because of my
gender and skin?

"Kamal"

At 26 you were too young to leave us,
too young to have the trials you faced, too
young to be a victim of a system that
waited for you to hurt others before
providing you the aid needed.

Neighbors, friends and family desperately tried
to come to your aid, to rescue you, to save you but
the system went deaf to pleas, the system
turned a blind eye, the system designed to help,
failed you. And rather than intervene

their inaction ushered you towards the grave.
Neighbors, friends, family and strangers mourn you today.

Today your injured family is nursing
physical wounds and emotional hurts
caused by the circumstances that led to your demise.
You were far too young, far too young to be
so troubled, far too young to have been
forgotten, far too young to have been
failed by the system but you will always be
loved, you will always be remembered,
you will always be treasured.

The turmoil has ceased, there will be no more
yelling, there will be no more wandering,
there will be no more internal warring.
You are home in Father's arms. Peace
is finally yours. Calmness now resides.

Those left behind will always mourn. Those
left behind will always remember. Those left
will use your life to build upon your legacy.
They will speak for those like you, they will
support those like you, they will support
others who are too young to be troubled, too
young to be forgotten, too young to be a
victim of the system. Your name, your life,
your story will provide healing for others.

Rest now dear one, rest now sweet son, you can
rest now Kamal and while you close your
eyes, we thank you for opening ours to the
plight of those that are too young.

"Ambien: Late Night Decisions"

Last night,
after I consumed both videos of
Philando's body being consumed
by the American system via
the armed hands of an
unsteady officer,
I surveyed my room
and looked for some
thing, any thing that
I too could consume or
that could consume me
and free me from this
American hell.

See, I grew up thinking
we should all get along,
that we are all equal
despite being raised during
the LA and Crown Heights riots
that suggested otherwise.
We are better than this,
we got past that,
this is in the past.
Today should be different.
But it is not.

Today this verdict demonstrates why Father's Day
is so damn complicated for black and brown people.
It's not because my dad sucked when I was a child
because his life sucked so much as a child, that
as a child, his childhood best friend was a bottle.

Father's Day was conflicting because
there's so many fatherless kids,
so many children of broken fathers
who are blaming their fathers
for getting locked up for trying to make ends meet
the only way they knew how,
illegal enterprise because
they were blocked from legal ways to provide
so, they got locked up for the first time or yet again…

the cycle self-perpetuating, once forces implemented it.

Father's Day is conflicting because
our brothers are killed when they inform officers that
they have a weapon so that the authority figure isn't scared
and they then are still executed by fear.
Another child scarred.
Another struggling single parent home.
Another subliminally overt message that
even when following the rules,
the victim is to blame.

See, last night that video reminded me
what life has always taught me,
it doesn't matter that I have worked
thrice as hard and have more degrees,
the system is designed for me
to only ever be an assistant,
always assisting, never being assisted.
How do I know this?
Because if you close your eyes right now
and imagine a top executive,
who do you see?
You most likely see the opposite of me.
You don't see me.
America doesn't see me.
They only have ever seen
property that needs to be subjugated.
A threat to be systematically castrated if not terminated…

This reality led me to last night's wish to consume
the whole bottle of pills like my dad consumed
whole bottles of liquid grain.
Because this world,
this reality,
weighed too heavily on his soul.
It now weighs too heavily on mine.

And last night,
I desperately wanted to be free of the role my skin
placed me in as an American…
so, I reached for that bottle of Ambien,
but removed only a half pill.

Used it to counteract the
sleep depriving anxiety
brewing over being black
that would have kept me up all night.
I couldn't perform at my thrice as hard level
if I can't shake the injustice of that night,
of tonight,
of each night.
So, I used the half dose to sedate myself,
to temporarily ease my mind of the hurt…
hoping that when I awake
I'd find myself refreshed
just
enough
to fight
further,
to demand my place in the face of this injustice,
to excel where assumed I'd fail…

They can mistreat me,
but they won't get my soul.
I won't be broken.
It may be designed
so that I can't win,
but I will never give in.

"A Question Was Posed"

Do racial matters find you
or do you seek them out?

The answer:
By virtue of my exterior
racial matters are attracted to me like
moths to flames, like pepper spray to
marchers, like batons to skulls, like
41 shots to a wallet, like
chokeholds to a loosey, like
an execution to skittles...
It comes to me whether I'm
working while black,
walking while black, dining
while black, driving while black,
going home while black,
attending school while black,
or simply existing
while black.
My black attracts it even
when I don't want it,
it comes to me when
I just want to exist like others...
I can't exist like others...
I can't avoid the rules of attraction.
I only get to decide how
or if I will engage it today.

"Small Talk"

Everything was going great
between the strangers,
it was all love and fellowship
until Section 8 was equated
to crime and Trump was
discussed as a cause of cheer.
Nothing else was said
but the fast friends became
polar strangers again.

"An extra shot of melanin means"

An extra shot of melanin means
1 bullet, 6 bullets, 7 bullets, 20 bullets, 41 bullets, 50 bullets being shot in your direction for walking home armed with skittles, for supposedly stealing cigars, for offering up a permit, for using a phone, for reaching for a wallet, or for celebrating nuptials with friends. It's your family receiving no justice, having no peace when the gun smoke clears.

An extra shot of melanin means
extra room made for you when you enter elevators as ladies clutch purses, extra quarters made for you when you fail a third grade test, and extra physical affection as officers halt your path to provide unsolicited frisking. It means extra time spent if found with solid forms opposed to powdered versions of the same substance. It means a harder sentence applied to an already harder sentence.

An extra shot of melanin means
creating the carbon filament, closed circuit security systems, blood banks, air conditioners, walkers and many more items even when patents were forbidden, when partners took the fame, when you are denied access to your own life-saving inventions. Or you are simply omitted from history books.

An extra shot of melanin means
red lined homes, predatory loans, excessive interest rates and being admonished for poor money management. It also means segregated housing surrounded by food deserts and smog, and then increased rents matching the pockets of gentrifiers ready to disgrace and displace you and your legacy.

An extra shot of melanin means
acting roles are only offered as house slaves, mammies, field slaves, thugs, beaten slaves, pimps, bleeding slaves, maids, and other domesticated servants or if lucky historic figures that were slain like King, X, Evers, or Turner... Any other role is deemed too farfetched, fantastical, scientifically fictional really.

An extra shot of melanin means
being called articulate or eloquent and labeled an erudite, knowing they mean "for a black person," especially when you did nothing

spectacular or out of the ordinary. You simply did not come off as aggressive, angry and brutish as media would have them believe.

An extra shot of melanin means
straightening your curl, unbraiding your tresses, cutting off your locks and keeping your hair trimmed. Removing all sign of ethnicity from your follicles in order to get a job, keep a job, or to even be respected. It means that nothing deemed "beautiful" looks like you unless it is used to fetishize your features. You, as you are, are never really seen.

An extra shot of melanin means
watching cabs pass you by to stop for another. It's being told you have to pay cash while others can swipe. It's being denied service because you look like someone. It's being ignored in some stores and followed in others; you can't possibly afford that establishment.

An extra shot of melanin means
being asked: What sport do you play? Did you hear about that rapper? How do you do that dance? How many children have you got? Can I touch your hair? Why is it called soul food and not southern? As if you are their happy and eager black ambassador or as if you have any interest in any of those things.

An extra shot of melanin means
that the GI Bill was historically implemented to keep you in a trade. It means Affirmative Action, a policy designed to help you, benefited white women most. It means your historic colleges are underfunded as are your high schools, middle schools and elementary schools.

An extra shot of melanin means
PTSD is passed down like a family heirloom and that you will be triggered with every new news report. It means dining on microaggressions for breakfast, lunch, dinner, and as snacks in between. It means always being hyper aware of your body and what it can mean to others; even slight movements can be deemed threatening, slight gestures can be a terminal offense.

An extra shot of melanin means
you have stereotypes placed upon you and overt and covert racism applied to you. You are a temporary savior when elections go right and everyone's scapegoat when things go wrong. It also means so much more, it means being so powerful, so self-assured, so

determined, so unwavering, so beautiful, so skillful, so creative that others feel the need to discredit who you are. But you know who you are, therefore they will never ever succeed.

An extra shot of melanin is
a gift, inspiring others with jealousy and envy over their desire for an extra shot of melanin.

"An Interpretation"

Life is black
beautiful skin
it's powerful,
exotic, unknown,
dangerous, it's
frightening to
some
too frightening
it's dangerous,
unknown, exotic,
powerful it's
skin
beautiful
black is
life.

"A Farewell Letter"

Dear World, America,
Racist Society, To whom
it may concern or apply,

I am writing you to say farewell.
To bid you adieu.
To make a graceful exit from stage right.
This is my resignation letter
from all things you, from this society,
from this overt and covert system
of oppression that you've been pressing

against my larynx since before
all the miracles came together
to form me, as you see.
I was never a willing pawn in your play,
just a chess piece plucked from the Continent
used for manufacturing your wealth,
whether in fields or from bullpen offices.
And I am weary of the game.
Wearier still of my role you've scripted and directed,
then you forced me to witness repeatedly,
repetitively showing me portrayals of brown skin
as slaves cakewalking,
as mammies catering,
as thugs being jailed,
as leaders being slayed,
as if to say my only place
in your wet dream is
chasing the dangling reward,
a place where I'm never reaching a pinnacle
but always only ever dangling at a precipice
needing your approval,
and dammit I no longer approve
and will no longer work to prove
my place
in this masterly designed race.

Shit, if a black president
wasn't enough to show you
that black excellence
is equally, if not more, excellent,
then what chance have I?
If all of our inventions
never got your attention,
if all of our intentions
are greeted with henchmen,
if all of our ascension
was beyond your comprehension
then you can skip giving me honorable mention
in the credits of this story.
I'm tired of displaying all my goods for you,
prostrating myself to you,
only for you
to leave my scenes on the cutting room floor,

another sacrificed pawn,
another skilled performance dismissed
in this crafted pre-
fabricated story.

I am not shucking,
jiving and
yes massa-ing anymore
in order for you
to win the next award,
the next battle,
to collect the next pawn.

I'm laying my chess piece down,
writing myself out if this script,
collecting my hidden computers and
tessering to Wakanda
where I am appreciated and
where I can just be free,
my throat no longer under
your oppressive shoe,
my hue no longer subject to your view.
So, to whom it may concern or apply,
our relationship is through
and I'm taking all my good stuff too.

Farewell, adieu,
parting is such a sweet
breakthrough
as will be my life once out
from under you.

What It All Means

"Morning Greeting"

Each morning Dread
seductively greets me
draped in silky reminders
of pressure, doubt,
condescension and highly
low expectations. And
whether I want it in my
personal space or not, it
claims me as its own,
embraces me in a way that
pins me to my bed and
whispers reminders
of all I hate and do not
wish to engage in. Dread
distracts my eager brain
until it slows and spins
into anxious panic, stealing
all confidence in my planned
productivity. I cannot fail,
though expected to. My heart
races at the thought of
succumbing to the gray
weight of this lover Dread…
but then I roll it off of me and
onto its side, realizing Dread
was only a mental rehearsal
and now I'm ready for
the performance. I passionately
kiss my partner farewell and
address the day. Nothing else
faced is nearly as bad
as our morning ritual.

"Split-Identity in a Minority War"

Warring parts of self birth palpitations
My existence defined as perverse
In- (and ex-) ternal interrogations
I'm cursed for being doubly diverse
Not knowing which fight in which to immerse
A portion of self I'm forced to denounce
Black woman life is deadly to traverse
Majority always plotting to pounce
Autonomy breeds confrontations
One or other, no self proclamations.

"So Much to Tell"

Let me tell you about my people,
my beautiful people,
my people that resided and presided
at the very origin of people,
my people who have since
been targeted for genocide
by other people, by "fairer" people.

Let me tell you about my
beautiful deep brown people
who helped establish all you currently
know and get stripped of their credit
every single day, yet they are
a people who still endure today.
Let me tell you about a people that
provided rhythm for all but are often
relegated to second best, even
in genres they originated... My people
were the original mathematicians and
scientists but now they fight for a spot
in the new and esteemed STEM fields;
after all, being anything more than
entertainment is not allowed here...

Let me, tell you, about my people,
my people who are so great
that other people emulate and even
appropriate everything about them,
everything but their pain,
everything but their subhuman rank,
everything but everything
that truly makes them
who they are forced to be
in this biased world everyday...

Let me tell you...
there is so much to tell you that
Texan history books are overtly
erasing, trying desperately to forget
but my people will not be forgotten,
we will not be silenced, even
when we can't breathe,
with our hands up, we scream
for attention, demanding recognition.

There is much I want to tell you
about my people who invented many
of your modern-day conveniences, but
when we tell our truth
it is deemed inconvenient.

I need to tell you, about my people that
fought and are still fighting for your rights
fighting for your rights to be fully
developing, equally respected,
human beings.
We are fighting for you
even when we fight alone.
We do it because even on this day,
others would have us relegated
to classifications of apes and
coons or 3/5 human,
but the reality is,
that if we are not okay,
if my people are not okay
neither are you.
Even if you don't realize it,

once our rights are stripped,
yours will be next,
so we fight against the nooses
around all of our necks.

My people
are royalty
always have been
always will be, even
if it is our crowns you refuse to see.
Langston, Maya, Sonia, Amiri,
Gil, Stacy Ann, and Saul all
speak to our beauty,
to our endurance, to
our legacy. I want
to add to their voices, I
want to tell you about
my people.

I need to share the story
of my people. It is a great
tale, a tale of struggle,
triumph and grace but
I can't tell it to you just yet.
I can't tell you because
they just silenced
#SandySpeaks.
Snuffed her light,
stopped her from speaking
like they stopped Martin
from preaching.
Silenced her like they
silenced so many others
before her and like they
will try to silence so many after.
They are actively erasing
our story at this very minute,
removing any truths inconvenient
to the tale they would like to spin.
They are Rush Limbaugh-ing my history,
Donald Trump-ing my plight,
Fox News-ing my existence
And I can not let this be.

I have to fight the erasure of my people,
this systematic genocide of my beautiful
brown skinned people cannot continue.
So unfortunately, I do not have that time
to pause and tell you about my people.
I wish I could but I must pick this
conversation up later, after I raise up
my fist and pick up this picket sign,
after I march tirelessly and vote loudly
so that my people will still have
the right to share, the avenues to share,
the ability to share, the story of our people,
without threat of death for sharing.

But if my protest is thwarted,
if by chance I am arrested
for taking part in this movement,
#ifidieinpolicecustody know
it was not of my own doing
But an attempt by them to silence me
an attempt at stopping me
from setting the record straight
about the story of my people.

"A Black Woman's Plight"

Ever the strong one,
she declined help,
refused to acknowledge
that she needed
medical assistance,
even when her body
poured tears from her eyes,
tears that were begging
for the attention that
her emotions refused
to connect to. Her body
was literally broken and
screaming for help but
she walked determinedly
into that meeting ignoring
pain; weakness was
never an option.

"Fibroids - A Black Woman's Strength"

As the monthly pain sets in, as
her leg begins to aches, and her
toes curl from the pain, as her
delicate and misshapen organs
rip apart, shedding lining and layers
and as her head begins to split
from the changes of chemicals
she thinks of her sisters, her sistahs
and wonder why it is black women,
a group that already is discounted
and forced to suffer in graceful silence
under the burden of their skin,
why is it that they are genetically
predisposed to baseball sized
growths and excessive hemorrhaging
crying rivers from their heart, bleeding
rivers from within and must still
grin and bear it. Any sign of weakness
is not allowed, it fulfills stereotypes,
so even in their own special agony
they summon all their strength and
fight through it to overcome it all.

"Statistically Speaking"

Two women,
followed the grid
along their breasts.

Both felt something.
A small mass.
Both sought help.

But it's here stories diverge.

One, though more likely
to have malignancy, will
also have greater odds
of survival, they will thrive.

The other, the least likely
of the two, is more likely to die.

The difference?
Their levels of
melanin.

Why? Why? Why?
Why is this diagnosis
a death sentence for only me?
Is it the money in my pocket,
or the fact that I'm less likely
to be believed, heard, listened to?
Is it that the quality of doctors
I can access will be suspect
or that they just won't care as much
about helping heal me.

Why? Why? Why?
Why is breast cancer
more likely to be a
death sentence for me?

"Half of Me"

With each new day that there is a catastrophic atrocity in the news, I am forced to put half of me to the side and pick up the other half's fight.

When reproductive rights are being attacked, white women demand that I march alongside them but I must fold up my skin and place it in storage for another day. Mums the word about being black. I'm simply a woman. Our women fight is the same; no dividing us with racial talk. Just fall in line and chant.

When a black soul is legally stolen by an authority figure, I'm again beckoned to fight, I must pack away my ovaries and march and protest on behalf of black men. I must fight for the humanity of my male kin; my job is to protect and defend. But I must not say her name, her name is irrelevant to the racial war roaring ahead…

But when will all white women and all black men fight for all of me? When will they fight for the battles unique to me. Fight for the inequity in medical care that increases my mortality, fight for real equality bringing my lower than white women wages up to white men pay rates, fight for protection against 11-minute-long vaginal cavity searches because drugs are suspected? When will the two halves of me unify to defend me? Why is the burden of everyone else's fights on my back? When will they finally have mine?

"Tone Policing"

As she skillfully switched
her tongue for special
emphasis, the perception
from the judging ears
vacillated between hearing
pleasing eloquent and
articulate sounds
to being disappointed
and turned off by the
unsophisticated choppy
noise and then returned
back to accepting the
non-threatening astute
erudite-like flavorless croon
when it so pleased them to,
all while missing the
message conveyed.

"Working while black"

After forced smiling,
yes ma'am-ing or sir-ing,
opinion swallowing,
doing without thinking,
taking on more,
breathing through insults,
pretending it isn't infuriating.
And after arriving early,
after a working lunch,
after regular hours,
after staying late,
after being more educated
and respected less,
she is spent.
There's nothing left
she's lost herself after
giving it her all.

"Entitlement - A New York Story"

My brown hips filled my orange MTA seat
next to the silver pole and spilled slightly
into the next. My neighbor's bigger brown hips
filled her seat and then some, leaving only
half of a seat between us. A pair of white male
hips filled the space between her and
the unforgiving train wall. Three hips
comfortably situated until a fourth set
sat in the laps of two. Her smaller yet
full seat size hips tried to squeeze
into the remaining half. Though vowing to take
only the edge she squeezed and squirmed,
and wiggled until my hips shifted and
my ribs met the railing. The other brown hips
were pissed and having no nonsense today.
There's no room for her end, in the end, but
the hips demanded that the others
accommodate her's... those white hips
were going to take a space where none was,
they were entitled to the half seat
even though they were not half sized...
Those already there didn't matter,
my ribs should be one with metal poles,
his hips should be pressed into the wall,
the other brown hips needed to shrink and
accommodate her precious frame. Rather
than be in pain, regardless of my torn brown hip
attached to a worn-down knee and a slow to
heal injured ankle, my hips rose rather than
raise ruckus... An onlooker pair of hips
called out the audacity of entitlement...
"Why should brown seated hips stand
so white able hips can sit?" My hips inhaled,
and exhaled, then offered grace, which was
counter the profanity justifiably offered
by the other brown pair...Then my brown
hips exited the train, headed towards better,
better than the scene that took place,
they were better than the entitled hips
that took the place in which mine were entitled.
My hips were deserving of better treatment

though they were not honored, not respected, not
acknowledged, just an inconvenience and
an impediment to her entitlement...
if only this were just a New York story...

"A Privilege I Do Not Have"

My medium brown crayon skin
does not allow me to walk through
New York City streets parading
myself in front of tourists, locals and
officers with a clutch bag with a
realistic gun embossed on the front.
What is a fashion statement for my
peach crayon-colored counterpart,
in the wake of a 58-murdered-people
lone wolf teroristic massacre, would
surely be my demise, as reaching
for my wallet would be confused with
reaching for more. I am not afforded
the privilege of being fashionable,
I'd get 41 bullets, my worst image
dredged up, and with tales spun about
how much of a miscreant I was,
all to accompany the photos of
riddled brown and red me in all my
insideoutness having been placed
on display like bodies from trees
in tomorrow's news. *I should have
never have had that purse* will be
the commentary heard, *I should
have never reached for identification
papers proving my emancipation,
I should have never breathed...*

"Micro-Isms"

In the throes of a polite
argument about police
brutality and modern day
racism with a younger
black woman, the older
white male, paused and
praised the older black
male for raising such a
"good" and "articulate"
young lady. The older
black male, though only
entering the debate
to offer unsolicited defense
for said daughter, took
the compliment as if
it was his to claim. Both
thinking they were doing
good, reinforced so much
harm. But this woman
knew definitively that
she needed absolutely
no approval, agreement,
permission, or defense
from either in the pair.
She was, she is and
she has had, enough.

"Futuristic Fiction"

I am looking forward to the day
when I am free.
And I don't mean the boss is out so I get to relax,
free,
or first day of a seven day vacation,
free,
I mean really
free.
I mean rich white
heteronormative, cisgender male
free.
I am waiting for the day where I am
Donald Trump kind of free.
Where nothing matters,
where I can change my skin orange,
cheat on my mate,
go into bankruptcy several times over,
break every rule,
blatantly and badly lie to people's faces
and still get the top spot and
the benefit of the doubt,
free.
That's the kind of freedom I want.
Now don't get me wrong,
I don't want to be white,
or male, or even rich,
but I also don't want
my exotic hair petted,
I don't want men assuming
I'll move for them,
I don't want to be charged
a pink tax for existing,
I just want to walk through my country
without fear of being called
a nigger, or a bitch,
or any other horrible name the majority
has deemed my brown, round,
female body with.
I want to know what it's like
to not be objectified,
vilified, and dismissed.

I want to really be free,
free from fears that driving,
BBQing, studying,
walking, sleeping,
swimming, dining,
shopping, or
breathing while black
is a crime punishable with death.
I just want to relax, exist,
and not worry about offending anyone
with the space my life takes.
I'm waiting for that day,
waiting for the day when I am
free.

"Still Can't Win"

With 25 Squares
And with a myriad
of possible answers
In today's game
I placed markers here:
- ✓ Blindness to color
- ✓ But isn't that reverse racism
- ✓ Indifference to difference
- ✓ I was taught not to be racist
- ✓ I'm an individual
- ✓ Not all white people
- ✓ Now, now, lower your tone
- ✓ Not my ancestors!
- ✓ Go protest differently
- ✓ Get rid of black on black crime
- ✓ One people, one love

And yet I was still
- o One precious teardrop

away from winning
Fragility Bingo

"I am tired."

I am tired of explaining to you why it is not okay for you to ask me to let you satisfy your curiosity about the coarseness of my hair. I am not your animal to pet. And I am tired of explaining how I can wash my hair without my locks unraveling. In fact, I am just fucking tired of my hair being an oddity to you.

But that's just a minor part of my fatigue. I am honestly just tired of being told I do not belong in my own country; the country in which I was forced to live, love and die for. I can't raise a flag on the fourth, because I just can not show pride about a country that has told me I was less than human, that I was property, that they can take my life at any moment, and that I should go back to whence they stole me from. To be full of pride, is to love my abuser and there's not enough fucking love left in me.

But I am really tired of having to explain to those that support this joke of a system as to why I'm pissed about the fact that my vagina and melanin justify the treatment I receive. You created this system to hold me hostage, so why is it my duty to explain to you or to convince you to love me? You have the power; it's clear that in this game, I am nothing, my children are nothing, my family is nothing, nothing but consumers you milk for every dollar then blame for their own condition, a condition you profit from. I get overlooked for jobs so that you can hire him… was it because you were afraid that my cramps would make me unreliable. Don't you know it is my cramps that prove I have more physical endurance than he… but that Y chromosome enters you into a boy's club that I can not compete in… And then when you do hire a double X, you hire the less melanated her over me, when I am the one with the actual degree. I am fucking tired.

I am tired of being told it is not always a race thing. I do not claim to own the market on oppression but I also understand it always boils down to haves and have nots and often times that can be attributed to the "other" syndrome, the fear of others that do not immediately burn under the sun. Let's stop playing this game and call it what it is… America's got a race complex… it is always about race even when your rose glasses or limited access causes you to dismiss every hue but yours…it's time to stop being so fucking blind.

I am tired of being told to stop being negative, to be softer, to play the game when it is the game that has kept me five steps behind. I am tired of working exponentially harder for exponentially less... I am fucking tired of loving in the face of hate. Everyone else gets to show their hate loudly and proudly but I am told to be graceful... Fuck that. I'm too tired for any more...

"Prayer Chain"

Lord, I need a spiritual intervention.
the type of intervening given
in answer to prayers Feliciana must have prayed
when she prayed for her descendants
to be free from their masters' clutches.
I need an intervention like ones her son Louis prayed
when he was shipped from Trinidad to the Carolinas,
all things around him tumultuously changed
and he called out for his spirit to be calmed.
I need that kind of intervention.
I require a spiritual and divine intervention
like the kind asked for in the prayers Chester must have prayed
when forced to decide between the North and the South,
freedom or serving his self-proclaimed owner.
I call for your intervening hand.
I need intervening like the kind Florence requested
as she entered a brave new world
where her children were legally free,
but were still seen as items, seen as property.
Honestly, I need a spiritual intervention
of the likes Annie sought when the north
had a renaissance that the south could only dream of,
that she could only dream of.
And my, oh my, do I need the kind of spiritual
awakening and intervening that led to the dreams
Arthur dreamt in hopes of better opportunities
for his children and their children and their children.
I need the kind of spiritual intervention my dad
marched for when in Washington, seeking equal jobs
and fair treatment as a human being...

Today I need to be the recipient of their spiritual
pleas for the Most High's mighty intervention.

And God, I need the spiritual intervention my mother experienced
when believing that her children
would be given grades they earned not just the lesser than
option imposed on her because of her skin.
I need the spiritual intervention that her mother,
Odessa, prayed for when the family-fracturing
migration north was deemed necessary.
I also need the spiritual fortitude Elora experienced
when having multiple children with limited means
while never receiving her promised restitution.
And I need the intervention Sarah
and her minister husband received
in response to their intercessory prayers prayed
as the world changed and vagrancy rules
became a coloreds only penalty.
I desperately need the spiritual
support and endurance Lettuce instilled in us
after seeking it every day while enslaved.
And Lord I need the spiritual intervention that
Lucinda must have prayed for and exhibited
as she posed for her master's photo.

I need this spiritual intervention,
the kind in which my foremothers
and forefathers prayed over me,
and for me, long before there was a me
and that today empowers me
to live and operate in excellence
despite the insidious descendant
of racism and slavery that has always
plagued my kin. It is the enemy that
bred me, raised me, and chased me
but won't break me as I resolutely
match its determined glares today.
I need this spiritual intervention.

"Dear Self"

Dear depressed and
helpless, hopeless me,

Thank you.
Thank you for not giving up,
for not swallowing those tempting
anguish-releasing pills,
for fighting just a bit longer,
for giving the world and yourself
one more chance.
Thank you
for the choice you made that night,
the choice you made to stay alive
despite being uncertain that you could thrive.
Your strength then, propels me today and
on all days deemed bleak, on the overwhelming days,
on the days I just want to crawl into myself and hide.
The fact that you chose to fight on
in the face of unceasing racial inequality
deeming your existence disposable and
choosing to face the unrelenting demons
inside your head eating at your heart
gives me strength today to know I can too,
that this iteration of me can and will prevail.
You made it through that soul-devouring night
so that I could fight today,
so that I can be here to fight today,
so, I thank you.
Thank you for never surrendering.
Thank you for leaning into God and others
and speaking your truth and owning and
embracing the necessity that is you.
Thank you for picking up that pen
and bleeding over the page
instead of drifting off to perpetual sleep.
Thank you for writing your story
so that I can recite it today,
so that I can be here
to make sure it is heard today.
Thank you.
Thank for showing me

that it's okay to feel pain,
to exist on a tumultuous plane, and
that moment was only for a moment
even if it felt like an eternity and
beckoned like it was a sweet destiny.
Thank you for ignoring the sleepy siren and
heeding the call to be present and
use that moment like the present it was
so that I can be here to share your story presently.
Thank you.
Thank you for that mustard seed of hope
that you planted
so that I could grow into today
and blossom tomorrow.
Thank you for giving me and future us a chance.
We will forever be indebted to you and
will forever appreciate you.
You are the strength that reminds us to endure.
Thank you for surviving that night,
thank you.

Thank you,
On behalf of me and future you

"A Gold Star Day"

I deserve a gold star for
letting the latest act of
stupidity by the latest
elected President not
create panic or anger
in me. And I deserve
another gold star for
staying away from the
latest posts about
the unarmed black person
executed by the police.
Nor did I spend too much
time mourning over
the young black college
graduate who was
pummeled to death
senselessly by a mob
of white men while
traveling to Greece.
This is why I fear traveling.
I instead spent the day
resting, and cleaning,
and binging on superhero
TV. Unplugging from
a traumatic reality is
sometimes necessary
in order to be just okay.

"Haiku on Being a Black Woman"

We watch News tonight
hoping not to see another
brown body abused

"Korryn's Final Stand"

She reached the final straw and
whether that straw broke her sanity
ushering her into a world of paranoid
illness or it pissed her off just enough
that no more fucks could be given,
I will never know. We will never know
but she had enough…

We will never know if it was disease
that led her to see stealing where
there was confiscating or kidnapping
where there was detainment, or if she
was tired of pretty words and called it
what it was, theft of property and the
disappearance of others without
the ability to notify loved ones. We
will never know. I will never know.

But we do know that while detained
she wrote notes to anyone who could
intervene begging someone to help.
"Help me" she wrote again and again
and truth be told, I am not convinced
that her pleas were any different than
the messages we send, the statements
I've made when I, when I just can't
deal with any more oppression, any
more mistreatment, any more injustice
orchestrated by our justice system…

I just can't be sure. We just can't be sure
if she was delusional or the clearest
minded of us all when she refused
to recognize an authority that refused
and refuses to recognize our humanity.

Korryn took her last stand. Gun in hand
refusing subservience, demanding
respect… and I can't help but respect
that. I am not cosigning her actions but
can certainly appreciate her request for

governance by an authority that doesn't
kill people that look like her kin for sport,
doesn't lock them up for wealth, does not
offer only secondhand citizenry... I
can respect that whether through clouded
perception or crystal vision she was
having none of that treatment anymore.

And though we will never know what that
last straw was or what was going on
inside her head, we do know she was
not the first to shoot. We know that
those officers never gave her the days
they've given others who barricaded
themselves. We know they put her
down. Silenced her permanently. We
know she defended herself until the end.

We know that she wasn't just an angry
black woman, that she can never be
deemed just an angry black woman, that
even in death she can never just be
dismissed as another angry black woman
but as one determined to live in freedom
or die seeking it. At 23, she boldly, bravely
unrepentantly made her last stand.

And we will never know what that straw was
but we know Korryn will forever be an
example, a cautionary tale of what
a people pushed to breaking, become.

"No Comparison but Similar Still"

He hung wearily from the branches,
sliced, bleeding, abandoned.
Holes savagely driven into his
bony appendages. His heavenly
crown stripped; replaced by thorns,
but He still uttered words of love,
worked until the work was done.

This is how the Messiah was treated,
so why should she in her tan skin,
with her wooly hair, expect anyone
to hear her plea or feel empathy
when she wails with sorrow from
the centuries of injustices suffered?

How can she expect a nation
to understand their freedom
from racism can only be gained
in emancipating her? Their liberation
from this consuming rage starts
in refusing to subjugate any longer.

Ending slavery on paper and
allowing her the right to vote
was not enough to save souls.
It was not a good enough deed
to bridge the gap between sin and
salvation. They must see her,
hear her, assist her, and resist
with her. Grace must be sought.

But these are those who use
His Word to unleash bile and to
spew hate, never heeding
the example displayed
on that cross on that Friday.
They misunderstand His purpose;
denying Him still. And though she
isn't He, though there is no
comparison to be made, she
finds herself existing similarly.

She like He, gives all there is,
provides, nourishes, supports,
guides, advocates for others
and is repaid with dismissal;
contributions used as sources
of humor and humiliation.
Her role is that of degradation.
She, left on display, in this play
aptly titled "America: Their Story".

She is not He. She will never be.
She is just following His lead.
She is just a small vital part
of His humanly faulty family;
the one who bears the wrath
of, and for, her weaker kin.

Why then would
they ever really
consider her plight,
when they never
truly or earnestly
appreciated His?

"The Answer is No"

A war against all women has been subtly waged
Necessity requires treaties across lines be formed
Actively seeking commonalities for a greater good
Therefore prayers, fellowship and communion are shared
Spirits and hearts are seen above the tone of one's skin
One voice in a fight against masculine oppression

But will I ever be deemed good enough to invite home?

To white standards, preferred outcomes are set
Talk of race disparities are deemed divisive
Other concerns relegated to the back again
No space for additional needs or other benchmarks
Vows of unity made, while still leaving some to march solely
Movements are co-opted, female minorities are whitesplained
Cracks in alliances appear, claims of unity a façade
But campaigns are won and wrongs prevented thanks to some

But will I ever be worthy enough for an invite home?

Fragility and privilege serve to silence others
Trust broken, once "common" goals achieved
Scripts are flipped when faults are pointed
Blood drips down the backs of those stabbed
Unity was only ever a ploy, race and other isms prevails
Lifelong sisterhood proved to be simply temporary

Will I ever be equal enough to be invited home?

"Rachel's Privilege"

No matter how much I do not want to,
no matter how worn down I may be,
I wake up,
I enter the world,
I arm myself against
all things that will come my way.
I prepare
for my hair to be touched by strangers.
I prepare
for my boss to show her lack of confidence
in my ability even though I am overqualified.
I put my headphones on so I cannot hear
the ignorance spewed about the character my skin implies.
I guard my heart from messages
that I will never be able to love my partner
like some fairer lady can.
I close my eyes to the images of beauty
that look nothing like me.
I try to operate in ignorance
of all the disparities I will face today, every day.
I start the day first,
end the day last,
and I try my best
to not be seen with chicken or watermelon
because I can't afford to feed the stereotype.
I cannot wash away the melanin of my skin
therefore, I have to fight to overcome
is the message received, even if I solicited none.
And even if I straightened my hair,
it would never be quite white.
I cannot change my identity with the tide.
The only time I get to be me
is in my home with no one around.
No tv, radio, or brainwashed kin.
My skin will not afford me to find peace elsewhere.
Your empathy with my blackness,
is simply sympathy, because your privilege
will always enable you with the ability
to walk away when it gets too real.
I don't get that privilege.

"Turn of Fortunes"

Dear Tomi,

I wish I could feel bad about your forced silence.
For your bosses to pay you to stop speaking once
you spoke your truth, must be a betrayal. It must
be tough to now be the snowflake you labeled others.
I wish I could side with you in sisterhood, as a
fellow woman silenced for voicing her opinion on
what she should be able to do with her uterus,
but I can't. I marched in Washington for women
like you who didn't realize what was at stake but
you've advocated so much against my right to exist.
You demanded that I protest in ways you deemed
appropriate when my life and existence were at stake.
You essentially said sit there and wage a silent protest…
be quiet… and now you've been quieted… told
your words, your experience, your life does not matter
when it shares dissenting opinions. I don't revel
in your turn of fortunes but I wonder if this will
even help you see how fragile your house is,
help you realize that as long as I can be treated
terribly with my uterus wrapped in black skin,
you too can fall out of favor, fall from grace just for
being you, for living in your truth… welcome
to a very small taste of my reality… am I still
a snowflake or the example of strength that you
must now replicate in the face of hate?

Welcome to reality…

"To John M"

For the record, I never thought of my body
as your wonderland when you sang your
sweet serenade from my iPod. And I am not
as offended as others might be. You've said
nothing surprising, only reiterated what my
own hip hop brothas have said, only tossed
more dirt on top of my name, so again you've
said nothing new. I know the truth, I am
the truth so your words had no real impact.
And personally, I never fantasized about
what it would be like to swim in a deep sea
of blankets with you. The way you've dogged
women of your past made you completely
unappetizing. But I have to applaud the fact
that you never hid your Elvis nature, you
always admitted that your musical style was
built on the backs of the black brothers
born to the same women you have no
interest in. I have to chuckle at your idiotic
retelling of your manly kiss, which only
highlights your repulsive behavior. And I
can't help but giggle at the fact that Mr.
Womanizer himself has a limp supremacist
penis when encountering a woman such
as myself. It's truly hilarious you see, so I
can't get angry, can't shatter your CDs, can't
delete my downloads like others have because
I'd then have to burn 90% of my rap CDs as well.
Must your beliefs discredit your musical ability?
Nope. But I make this suggestion:
by all means go get stoned, turn off
the lights and the telephone, but
don't get high again, right before speaking
bluntly into an interviewer's microphone.

"Why I Can't Date White"

While I appreciate kind gestures
such as doors held, meals paid,
and you walking on the outside,
I do not want it if it's only because
I am a trophy and not a treasure.
I do not want it if the goal is to
check off fat and/or black woman
on your sexual scavenger hunt.
I am not here for massa fantasies,
loving me equally should be the goal.
I don't want anything if it is not out of
appreciation for me as your partner
but it is done as a display of ownership.
I deserve genuine intentions,
not just because you'd genuinely
like to see me piss off your family
by my overwhelmingly brown presence.
I am not for your manipulative uses
I require and only accept authenticity.

"Why am I still single?"

I'm single because of daddy issues, black statistics, my weight, bad dudes/fuckboys, celibacy, and NYC sucks. I am still not taken because I am a black woman, media says I'm unlovable, my natural hair and lack of makeup makes me too much of a beauty rebel and because dudes are intimidated by my degrees and my power. But I am really still single because despite all of that, my standards are too high to settle for just anyone who thinks that I'll be grateful for their attention simply because the above makes me less typically attractive, the fact is they should be grateful for mine. So, I guess you can say I'm single by choice. Now that I've answered, will you stop asking?

"The Odds"

The odds are good
that I will be single
into perpetuity.
Stats suggest that
not only am I failing
to reproduce, but
my marriage rates
are severely reduced.
The African-American
population is headed
for a decline and it will
be all my fault,
talk shows continue
to discuss how unlovable
I am as if this is new news.
But it is not.

And I am not
fully or solely to blame.
Don't forget
that he didn't make it to 18,
though here I am at 38.
He was gunned down
in a turf war or
a cop misidentified him
as target practice.

And if a premature death
were not his fate,
while I climb the ladder
as far as my skin
and this ceiling will allow me,
he climbs prison walls
because driving a nice car,
carrying weed,
being addicted,
fighting for his life,
acting in concert,
being near someone,
looking like someone
led to years in confinement

stymying his ability
to keep pace
in this rat race.

Or if he is free
to be left to his
own devices,
my education
is deemed
intimidating,
my power
diminishing,
my caring
nagging
so others are chosen.
I'm bypassed for others
who are deemed more
passive, nicer,
ladies who cook more,
clean more,
cater more
than time ever allows me to.

Or there's the others
who loves physically
loving us but
also loves
tearing us apart.
Whether their tools
are used verbally,
physically, psychologically,
the goal is to
lessen our shine,
securing our place
as secondary.

And though I love
my brothers enough
to support them still,
to guide and encourage
and march for them still.
I still love myself enough
to love myself by myself

if that's the only love
I am offered from
perspective mates.

I can't love men,
long expired or
who don't or can't
love me healthier
and who refuse
to defend me
like I defend we.

I hope I am wrong,
but the odds
are good
I'll be single
into perpetuity.

"But Do You Hear Me?"

I hear you.
And I can not ever forget you.
Your names and stories
exist in the very essence
of our membranes.
Not one child with melanin
crosses the adulthood threshold
without being told the tale of Emmett Till,
the teen murdered for allegedly
whistling at a white woman.
And before him there were nine
who lost their lives or livelihoods
over the lies of two who
screamed rape on a train.
The case against Haywood,
Clarence, Charlie, Andy, Roy,
Olin, Ozie, Willie, and Eugene
set records and almost tore
the north and south apart,
but even before this story unfolded,
a whole town, a black haven,

our Wall Street was set ablaze
because a white elevator operator
falsely screamed foul play.
Dick Roland and many others
lost their lives that hot night.
So, I hear my brothers who grew up in NY
with the Central Park 5.
The victim didn't point fingers
but still the futures of Korey,
Kevin, Raymond, Yusef, and
Antron were stolen anyway
so trust me when I say
I hear you.
Accusations have never
been the friend of brown skin
but did you hear me?

See, while I can appreciate
the knee jerk response to say
"not me, I'm not like him,
we need due process before belief"
I wonder do you hear me?
Because to me it sounds like white people
after another black slaughter…
a hashtag that inspires black people ire,
#notallwhitepeople but
when it comes to sexual assault
you loudly proclaim #notallmen
and expect me to not feel hurt.
Again, I say,
I hear you.
Accusations have never been
the friend of brown skin
but did you hear me?
Do you hear me?

During this time when women
are shouting and crying "me too",
are you listening or
backing away saying
"not me" and asking for proof
opposed to just listening?
As a black person I appreciate

the request for due process,
too many have had their lives
snatched away by lies
but I lay in bed terrified
that I will never heal from the men
that forced me into the #MeToo sorority.

Me too, and I'm not just referencing the times
I've had to correct guys
for speaking only to my breasts
or messaging me about the things
they'd like to do to me before
they ever said "hi."... Me too
because a bus driver grabbed my breasts
while picking up and dropping off passengers.
Me too because
I was so shocked
at what he did, that I told no one
but blamed myself for granting his request for a hug.
Me too because
I didn't say anything
when my partner, without my consent,
removed the condom.
I knew something was wrong,
something was different,
I cried from the violation
I felt and couldn't name
and he blamed me for killing the mood.
Yes, me too.
Me too because my date,
that I thought I was safe with,
dropped his pants
when I made it clear I wanted to go home.
And rather than seeing it as sexual misconduct,
I blamed myself for being there.
Who could I tell?
Who would listen?
And me too because
a guy bigger than me
stood between me and the door
and me too
because after many no's
I acquiesced.

I gave in under duress
and fear and
blamed myself
until I finally was brave enough
to share my story with the police.
But being a victim of date rape,
while trapped in a tiny room
with a judgmental man,
telling me it sounded like my fault,
terrified me back into silence.
But I can't be silent.
I can't be silent any more.
Three of the four were brothas.
Only one of the four ever admitted fault.
They all live their lives freely
and I,
I live imprisoned.
I have so many safeguards
around myself
physically and emotionally.
I stand in crowds checking faces for him,
I tell mutual friends that to him I don't exist,
I can't take a cab without making sure he's not the driver.
I live in fear
and will never get justice
but I do get,
"well can you prove it?"

Deeds done in the dark
are done in the dark
so that they can remain
in the shadows of the dark.
So the boys club prevails
when we are asked,
when I am asked
what I wore,
why did I stay,
did I say no,
why didn't I go,
tell me the details and I'll tell you if it was rape,
people lie you know...

I can't prove it,

I can't justify my actions
but they still took,
And gave a lifelong membership in
#MeToo…
I'll never prove it and
the fraternity will never be on my side,
they will never listen
because history has dictated so,
they are so afraid
of being slain again,
they can't hear me cry, me too…
Me too……
Me………
Too.

"Happiness"

When compared
to others, it feels
unattainable,
impossible,
and elusive.

When it is
not compared,
it is accessible,
attainable,
constant, and
yours for the taking.

It all depends on
where and how
you seek it out.

"As a Child"

I used to dream about
what it would be like
to leave my body and
travel the world. What
would I see? What would
I experience if I wasn't
tethered to this flesh,
if my spirit wasn't trapped
in the layers of brown
that was me. My spirit
yearned to be free
of what others saw when
they saw me. What would
life be like when viewing it
through non-myopic eyes?
What would the experience be
if the skin was a lighter hue?
I wanted to be free
to feel it all... And now
decades later my spirit
feels the same yearning.
My soul eagerly wants to
be free of the brown. I'd
love to swap places
with someone with paler skin.
Have them reside in a body
in a country where they
have no value. Would they
survive or implode? Would
they be overwhelmed
by the hateful stares?
Would they be able to grin
and bear it through the insults
and would they be able
to pretend that there was a
compliment in that comment or
would they still operate
with a perceived privilege?
And if I too were able to land
inside the body of a corporate
and upwardly mobile male,

would I be shamed for wanting
to flip the system on itself
by hiring those that didn't
look like me, by challenging
the norms? Or while entombed
in this other skin, would I finally
feel so safe, so free that I'd
forget to speak up for those less
privileged than me? What would
I value or what would the value
of me be if this childish wish
became actual reality?

"Vitiligo"

My skin is the manifestation
of the war raging in my psyche.
It highlights the internal struggle
that transports me back to that
icy salty waterway that marked
my fate and imprisons me still.
My African DNA is under siege
by that which massa injected
into grandma again and again
and again for generations. His
DNA lightened my kin but that battle
still rages within and is violently
evidenced by the blotches on my skin.
My brown is being attacked by white.
My brown…my brown helps proudly
separate me from the monotone
masses. My brown is that drum
that my heart beats to, it's the joy
that inspires my feet to movement,
it's my native tongue, my curly
hair and my voluptuous curves.
It's my family that was ripped
away, enslaved, stripped; it's the people
that stained the cotton red, that sang
the songs of joy, hope and freedom
just to sooth the whip created aches.

My brown matches my kente patterns;
it's the part that holds onto the memories
of indigenous kin. My brown is a testimony to
the struggle, the faith, the endurance
needed to survive the past and
make it into today… but even in today
it is not accepted, even in today my
inner workings battles itself.
Despite my protest, my body,
my DNA is betraying me…
Every day the blotch extends, every
day that I work, play, learn, study, I
accept the culture, the histories, legacies
and ways of being that pale in comparison.
Every day my tongue grows a bit more
distaste for my soul filled cooking and
craves the all mighty American hotdog
and cracker jacks. Every day I
subconsciously internalize the fact
that in order to be a successful black
person in America, I must be closer
to massa's complexion, I must exclude,
deny, gentrify myself, sell off bits and
pieces of my heritage and ethnicity,
until the disease has full control. Every
day my feet forget what it felt like to walk
the paths with my pail of water. Every
day I am reminded I was never from there…
there, I am only of here. My blood bleeds
red, white, and blue and in order to fulfill
my own dreams I must let this skin disease
overcome my original DNA, to erase
the songs inherently tattooed on my heart.
I must let this go, I must feast on more
hotdogs and soda pop, letting them fill me
with media that will devour my innards and
replace it with something more socially
acceptable. Each day here, I feel as if
I must let my brown lose this battle…
but I can't, that brown is still there,
it's still fending off the washing away
of ethnicity. Instead I must find a place
within myself where there is peace

with the pieces and blotches that
embody me. Both the light and the dark
are part of me and if I do not sooth
the war raging in me, on me, and around me,
I may lose all traces of who I used to be.

"Thoughts on Colorism"

At the conception of you,
He reached into his Crayola box
full of many natural hues of brown,
a box with an endless number of shades,
each bearing slightly different undertones
and tints but all essential parts
of his brown rainbow.
The spectrum extends from
the very softest shades of beige
to the richest ebonies imagined.
There's terrific tans and
magnificent milk chocolates.
And as He conceived of you
He reached in and picked
the perfect you shade,
the crayon named,
after you,
designed for you,
inspired by who you would be
as He dreamt up you.
Made sure it was the most perfect
of hues for his reflection.
He then painstakingly
colored in his creation,
was certain to stay within the lines and borders
that belonged uniquely to you.
Colored you in as only He knew you should be,
so how is it in your finite human wisdom
that you decided you were wiser?
Why are you destroying your perfect shade,
rubbing toxic creams,
ingesting false images,
destroying his vision of you,

opting for a ghastly unnatural hue.
Didn't you know He designed you perfectly?
Then why remove your color
in order to have a better view?
Didn't you know that you were best
when He designed you?
Don't you know you
weren't just his creation,
but his reflection which you've now marred
in bleaching more than just individual scars?
How could you im-perfect his perfection?
How could you not love the skin you are in
simply because He blessed another
with their very own shade?
Yours was a gift to you.
Please love it as He loves you.

"Black Girl Magic"

I've got that black girl magic,
that thing
that makes others wonder
just how I
did it... It's magic you see,
see
magically I endure. But
actually, I
do so much more, I
set
standards, break records and
create
styles you emulate.
You may
think you set the standard
but sweetie
it is my lips and hips
on which
you spend money to replicate.
It's my
hair that you love so much,
my hair

that you so much would love
to have
that you ridicule it simply
because you
just can't get it right. I'm sorry
that your
magic just ain't that tight.
See I've
got black girl magic,
that magic
granted by God to
make it
through the ignorance
and hate
you like to spew. He enables
me to walk
with my head straight,
there's no
shame altering my stride,
no fake
in my gait, nothing but black
girl magic
swagger, the power of which
makes you
stagger. You won't see me
fall or fail,
you won't see me sweat
under your gaze,
your hate is just haze,
this black girl
has got magic for days.
I've got
that black girl magic that really
isn't magic
at all, it's just a determination
to rise above
but it is magic to you
because
you've not ever understood
the complexity
and power of this person within
your view.
And that's perfectly fine,

my black girl
magic will continue to shine
because
every cell of my body, every
thought and
every action is just that divine.
Yep, I've got
that black girl magic,
that is all
types of black girl
fantastic!

"Silver"

She had flowing silver locks.
It cascaded from her roots
down to the small of her back
like the fountain of knowledge.
Its aura was that of wisdom,
of a profound existence, of a
life of devotion to Life. And my
short dark-haired self simply
wanted to sit at her feet and
hear her testimony, discuss
her philosophies, learn her
histories and admire a life
dedicated to Him. Her hair
inspired me to learn, to live,
and experience all that I can
like this woman had. She had
a beautiful mane of shimming
silver that I can only dream
of growing and having one day.

"What It All Means"

Two X chromosomes with an extra shot of melanin means
having an impossible beauty standard applied to you as you are told
to tame your natural mane in order to pass, to get promoted, to be
attractive, to be accepted.

Two X chromosomes with an extra shot of melanin means
having to suppress the needs of half of yourself when interacting
with either the double X or melanated communities. You are to
bolster numbers but your specific issues are never to be addressed.

Two X chromosomes with an extra shot of melanin means
being told "you remind me of Sandra Bland" while pulled over by
flashing lights and having to pretend as if your life wasn't just
threatened.

Two X chromosomes with an extra shot of melanin means
being cat called and told to smile when you just want to be left alone
and then standing strong while you're called a bitch because you
failed to respond with docility. In your mind you hope that that's the
only penalty you pay, that he won't shoot you because his ego was
too fragile to handle your rejection.

Two X chromosomes with an extra shot of melanin means
being told your educational and career pursuits make you absolutely
unlovable. *How dare you not focus on baking bread and babies? Oh,
the gall you must have to have other ambitions and demand a healthy
love!*

Two X chromosomes with an extra shot of melanin means
developing growths the size of coins, baseballs, or cantaloupes in
your uterus, hemorrhaging every month, and then smiling through
the pain that makes you pray for death while you are stuck working
all day; the bills must be paid.

Two X chromosomes with an extra shot of melanin means
being called President TJ's mistress when you were his rape victim, it
means your curves are a museum exhibit, and your stolen genes cure
them all.

Two X chromosomes with an extra shot of melanin means realizing that office politics dictate that there can only being one great woman of color, so your sistah friends at work are also your greatest competition. For you to propel yourself forward, you must hold your kin down.

Two X chromosomes with an extra shot of melanin means ignoring and overcoming it all, owning your shine, crowning yourself each day and being the queen you know you are. It's seeing your two X chromosomes with a shot of melanin as a blessing and badge of honor. Only few can survive the violence, the pressure, and the imposed blood sacrifice that you are exposed to on the daily and still emerge tough and radiating like the diamonds embedded in your ancestral land. It means this and so much more, it means you must and that you will thrive on!

Epilogue

"Black and Women"

They can try,
but they will fail.
See, rather than rage,
rather than dole
deserving hurt,
she flips the script
with her wit, vowing
never to let them see
her sweat or stressed.
She masks pain with smiles,
uses it as fuel
for greatness.
After all, their desire
for parts of her
is a testament
to her majesty.
Any attempt at taking
the whole of her
would make foolish
Icaruses of them.
They can try,
they will fail.
Her brilliance inspires
and scorches.
She is too radiant
and alluring,
too flawless
and faultless,
too determined
and powerful,
too resilient
and unbreakable
for others to ever
succeed in diminishing
and dismantling
all she is just
for their mortal
and greedy gain.
Black and women

can try, but they will fail.
They have tried,
and they have failed.
Black Woman,
a woman who is black,
will always prevail.

About the Author

As a young child, there was nothing Dara Kalima hated more than writing, but at the age of nine she was introduced to poetry and that hatred quickly became love. At 16, she started to acknowledge and honor her artistic inclinations. She became a founding member of the Creative Arts Team Youth Theatre and simultaneously started writing poetry on a monthly basis.

Dara holds a BA in Literature with a concentration in Drama Studies from SUNY Purchase. She later received her MA in Educational Theater from NYU and a MPA from Baruch College.

Dara performed on several stages across New York City including Bowery Poetry Café, the Nuyorican, Bronx Museum's Boogie on the Blvd and Mike Geffner's Inspired Word. She was also featured on WBAI's Perspectives hosted by the late Luis Reyes Rivera.

In 2015, Dara released her debut book, *Black Man, Black Woman, Black Child* which was a poetic exploration of what it could mean to be an African American in the United States. Two years later she released her second book, *Casualty of Love: A Poetic Journey From Butterflies to Broken and Back* which exposes her experiences as a sexual assault survivor. *Two X Chromosomes with an Extra Shot of Melanin* is the final book in this triptych of work inspired by current events and news cycles as she explores her vantage point from the intersection of black person and woman in a time of political unrest and activism.

Dara believes in addressing the difficult and taboo topics to create discussion, promote healing, and encourage critical thought within her community and across cultures. Dara believes that it is necessary to use her craft to speak for those who cannot yet do so. She is always up for a good conversation but beware, you may plant the seed for her next poem.

www.ingramcontent.com/pod-product-compliance
Lightning Source LLC
Chambersburg PA
CBHW032001080426
42735CB00007B/470